A Pedagogue's Romance

A Pedagogue's Romance
REFLECTIONS ON
SCHOOLING
Second Edition

KRISHNA KUMAR

OXFORD
UNIVERSITY PRESS

OXFORD
UNIVERSITY PRESS

Oxford University Press is a department of the University of Oxford.
It furthers the University's objective of excellence in research, scholarship,
and education by publishing worldwide. Oxford is a registered trademark of
Oxford University Press in the UK and in certain other countries

Published in India by
Oxford University Press
YMCA Library Building, 1 Jai Singh Road, New Delhi 110001, India

© Oxford University Press 2008

The moral rights of the author have been asserted

First edition published in 2008
Second edition published as paperback in 2015

ISBN-1 3: 978-0-19-945547-8
ISBN-10: 0-19-945547-3

Typeset in ITC Veljovic STD 10.5/13.6
by Sai Graphic Design, New Delhi 110 055
Printed in India by Replika Press Pvt. Ltd

for
Professor Yash Pal

Contents

Acknowledgements

The publisher acknowledges the following for permission to include articles/extracts in this volume.

India International Centre Quarterly for 'A Pedagogue's Romance', 28 (1), Summer 2001; 'A Memory of Coming to Life', 29 (3 and 4), Winter 2002–Spring 2003; and 'The Woman with a Broom', 26 (3), Monsoon 1999.

Journal of the Krishnamurti Schools for 'Teaching Peace', no. 10, July 2006.

Economic and Political Weekly for 'Freire's Legacy', 14 November 1998; and 'The New Politics of Education', 6 December 2003.

The Book Review for 'A Child's Swaraj', January–February 2000; and 'Let Us All Blame the Teacher', XXIX (10), October 2005.

The Times of India for 'Remembering Earthworms'; 'Future Girls'; 'Watching as Work'; and 'Lotus Syndrome'.

Seminar for 'Democracy Without Democrats?', issue 481, 1999; 'Adolescent India', issue 563, 2006; and 'Crafts at School', issue 523, 2003.

Hindustan Times for 'Understanding Women'; and 'Computers and Children'.

The Hindu for 'Two Memoirs of a Sporting Event'; 'Colour of a Girl's Skin'; 'Reading is Basic to Democracy'; 'Their Universities,

Our Universities'; 'Learning from *Iqbal*'; and 'Green Schools in a Greying World'.

The chapter 'Metaphors of Innovation' is a revised excerpt from a talk delivered at a workshop on 'Mainstream Innovations' organized by the Social Initiatives Group of ICICI Bank.

Centre for the Advanced Study of India(CASI), Philadelphia, U.S. for 'Cultural Context of Girls' Education'.

Introduction

How to write about education has always seemed to me a greater problem than *what* to write. I have been convinced ever since I started writing that the real challenge is to make the reader more demanding. Generalized writing about education inevitably takes the form of demagogic criticism. It is marked by supreme withdrawal from responsibility—to explain why a problem might persist—and freedom from the awareness of being an accomplice. That kind of writing always ends by providing great solutions too, for who doesn't have solutions to offer for India's educational problems?

Unless one gets into the daily details of education, there is hardly any point adding to the vast ocean of writing already available, especially in the form of reports. By details I mean what goes on inside education—inside the school gates and behind classroom doors, inside offices where decisions are taken or avoided, in training colleges, inside the covers of textbooks, and inside the vast, clandestine apparatus of the public examination system. It is this inner world of education that has always interested me, and I have been intrigued by its absence in much of Indian writing on education. There are exceptions, of course, especially now when a growing number of young scholars have started assiduously peeping into what

Michael Apple correctly called the 'black box', alluding to the everyday disaster that institutionalized education symptomizes in many parts of the world.

The selection of shorter essays this book offers is not intended for an exclusively academic audience. These pieces represent my desire to address the general reader who worries about education and wants to understand why it is in such poor health. From the point of view of this reader, it is truly puzzling that something with such incredible social potential should remain so stuck and moribund. The puzzle can be solved if we agree to distinguish between education as a concept and education as a system. When we engage with the concept or idea of education, we feel emotionally aroused, for education does evoke the prospect of a better, improved life in the future. Philosophers such as the Buddha and Plato have offered to humanity a vision of how, or what kind of, education can build and sustain a good society. Writing on the idea of education in this vein adds precious little to the already existing literature unless we spare some thought for education in the other sense, namely, its *system*. Our present system of education has evolved since the middle of the nineteenth century.[1] To think about the system is deceptively easy, for it is all around us and looks so obviously poor and unreformed to most of us. Its state of health hits us especially at the time our children are seeking admission to a nursery or college, or are about to face an examination. To analyse these chores in a precise manner, and at the same time stay in touch with the first meaning of education, that is its idea, is what I find challenging whenever I sit down to write.

Any attempt to meet this challenge makes one instantly aware that children's daily educational experience is not entirely the school's or the teacher's doing. There is a world

[1] I have traced some facets of this story in my study of colonialist and nationalist ideas in *Politics of Education in Colonial India*, Routledge, New Delhi, 2014.

surrounding the school that enters it in ways not all of which are subtle, yet it is easy to ignore them when we focus attention on how schools are running or how teachers are doing the job assigned to them. The world I am referring to constitutes powerful agencies which relentlessly shape the child's mind and behaviour. These agencies are so diverse and omnipresent that we can hardly enumerate them all. Where would you start and how would you distinguish? Television, for example, is an obvious choice among the agencies which exercise a great amount of influence on our children, but we can hardly separate television as a medium from what it shows, whether it is a scene from the parliament, a battleground in some remote country, or the advertisement of a new product. All such material, as well as the manner in which it is presented, shapes our children's perceptions and state of mind. Television edits reality, in highly problematic ways, but the character of the reality itself cannot be denied. Childhood is a stage of life when receptivity is strong and awareness is weak. The little child ends up engaging with everything, real or virtual, without distinction. It is customary and correct to call childhood a formative period of life, but this label seldom reminds us that the effort schools and teachers consciously make to educate children is intersected every evening by all that happens in the wider world and gets represented through the medium of television. Canadian economist-philosopher, Harold Innis, saw the technology of communication used in any period of human history as a *primary* force, shaping economic and cultural choices and the social order itself. The pervasive influence of communication technologies on how we think about learning and education has not been fully recognized. Some people occasionally worry about television and the Internet these days, but most of the time we bow to the inevitability of technological progress, and many of us begin to appreciate its utility for children and their education. Turning to a different facet of the world surrounding the school, the role that orally transmitted memory plays in shaping children's perceptions of the past and the future is ignored when people judge the impact of education. The point is that people construct the world in radically divergent ways with the help of their own imagination, and institutionalized education does not always manage to make them aware of their constructions.

The shorter writings collected here have been chosen randomly to encapsulate my professional concerns about education. In our society, education is not regarded as a serious profession. Teaching, which comprises the heart of education, has a poor status, especially if you teach children as opposed to youth. The poverty of our system of education has everything to do with the powerful value system which motivates both society and state to deny professional status to the teacher of young children. The fact that more women are now opting for school teaching compounds the problem. Women suffer from a major cultural bias to begin with, and the job of a nursery or school teacher does precious little to counter that bias. But it is not just the teacher of young children who has low professional status; those who train teachers fare no better. Indeed, teacher training can be quite accurately described as the centre of India's educational depression. In an ethos which gives increasingly greater priority to material status and power, how teaching can gain at least some of the value it deserves, is a big question. The larger questions of finding adequate funds for education and investing energy and money in reforms are equally important.

These questions are so intricately intertwined with political, economic, and cultural conditions that all answers look academically unsatisfactory. A decade ago, the National Council of Educational Research and Training (NCERT) mobilized an unprecedentedly widespread interest and participation across the country to prepare the National Curriculum Framework (NCF) (2005) which attempts to answer a good number of common questions on desirable options. This consensus document also aroused considerable curiosity because its acceptance as a professional roadmap cut across political divisions and regions. Even as the familiar shadows of bureaucratization in the public system and commercialization in the private realm lengthen, we must continue to exercise our right to imagine a different and better system of education.

I have chosen to call this book *A Pedagogue's Romance* because only romance looks capable of freeing us to imagine radical reforms. I could have called this book a teacher's romance, but teachers too, like planners, seldom have the time to imagine. Romance has been defined as a genre which allows us to move away from reality with the force of love and chivalrous concerns. The first set of essays will enable the reader to see a point in my 'pedagogy of hope', to borrow a phrase from Paulo Freire.[2] My analysis of his legacy forms the only lengthy piece in the opening section, all others being memoirs or sketches of life with the young. The second section deals with the world which surrounds the school and imposes constraints on the potential of education. Some of these constraints are historical; others are of a legal or political kind. Can the system of education soften these constraints after mindfully acknowledging their force? Essays included in the last section respond to this question. My hope is that the selection I have made will interest solution-seekers as much as the reflective reader. Over the recent two decades or so, the former have gained greater visibility and say; the latter kind of reader has receded into the margins of public life. I expect the new paperback edition of *A Pedagogue's Romance* to redress this imbalance among its readers.

---

[2] *Pedagogy of Hope*, Continuum, New York, 1997.

Colours and Shades

1

A Pedagogue's Romance

In early October 1994, the number of people spitting on the streets of Delhi suddenly declined. The garbage dump across from my house, behind the hostel for post-graduate (PG) women, was covered in a thick layer of gamaxin powder. Its sharp, limy smell gave an extra edge to the stench of DDT, which was everywhere. As I walked past Gandhi Bhawan, I saw two students looking like militants on television, with handkerchiefs masking their faces below the eyes. I had heard the rumour that in the PG Men's hostel, an Iranian student had reported a boil on his back. He had been taken to the hospital in Kingsway Camp, and now there was no way for him to get out of it, even if he applied for help from the Iranian embassy. A Muslim trader had apparently jumped off the *neem* tree near his window in this hospital, to death.

News of this kind instilled the same sense of fear that the residents of Pune must have felt during the plague of 1895. The Epidemic Diseases Act, passed by the British in 1897, still unamended more than a hundred years later, was now invoked by the Delhi municipality. Panic is not the right word to describe the feeling conjured up, although panic was part of it. A friend in the transport business had purchased hundreds of tetracycline capsules to distribute among his drivers. He was apparently in panic—but underneath his efforts was the common scare of compulsory hospitalization by the government if you were found with the symptoms of plague.

The terror of plague provoked many changes. That morning I noticed no one spitting around the botanical garden. In the absence of that loud, preparatory sound which men make a few seconds before they are about to spit, it became an unusually pleasant morning for a walk despite the smell of DDT. I say 'men' because the women who walk don't spit. A couple is walking quietly a few steps ahead of you; that familiar roar emanates from the man's throat, but the woman walking beside him doesn't so much as notice. Obviously, she is used to it, living with that man and walking like all other couples who go round and round the garden. Why have I not got accustomed as she is to all the spitting around me? If only I could take it as part of my morning scene, along with the noise that crows make when they get up, and the gleaming trunks of young teak trees along the path, I would be perfectly happy.

The roots of my discomfort lie, I suppose, in my professional mindset. As a pedagogue I am always looking for ways to improve things, especially human behaviour. That is why it makes no sense to me why, in the highly educated environment of my university campus, I should find so many people every morning who spit so readily: they are not part of the university I remind myself, in the hope of seeking solace. Their Ikons and Lancers are parked outside the gates where enterprising fruit sellers stand with overpriced papayas and custard apples. They can distinguish their customers from the odd teacher or student who walks beside the businessman from Kamala Nagar and the markets beyond. But it is hardly true that teachers and students don't spit when they want to. They do, but they are less raucous, that's all.

Mahatma Gandhi was the ultimate pedagogue. He understood the problem well, and he thought that by using it as part of a political joke he would solve it. I have seen how this technique works when applied to otherwise suffocating situations, like the Emergency: Popular jokes about Sanjay Gandhi gave people both relief and courage in those grim days. Mahatma Gandhi's joke about spitting inevitably focused on how to throw the British out. If all three hundred million Indians spat together—the emphasis was on together—they could drown the empire, Gandhi said. The pedagogic intent of that exhortation amazes me, especially how it conveys Gandhi's derision for colonial rule and his awareness that the real challenge for Indians was unity: the joke tries to turn an old weakness into a strength; that's what makes it a pedagogue's romance. As it happens, Gandhi's plea did not work. We continued to spit individually, and Gandhi had to find other ways to exasperate the British. The habit of spitting—Gandhi's real target—proved stronger than the empire. Pedagogues who want to do better than Gandhi must devise bigger incentives.

Legislators prefer deterrents to incentives. In December 1999, the Goa legislative assembly passed a law, which makes spitting in public a punishable offence. Anyone found guilty will have to pay a fine of Rs 1,000. My first reaction to the news of this law was admiration for the legislators of Goa! They had shown remarkable good sense and courage in choosing the obnoxious habit of spitting as the subject of India's final legislation of the twentieth century. At the beginning of the century, Gokhale had failed to persuade imperial legislators to make primary education free and compulsory. Gokhale's bill is still pending, but we did better on other difficult issues like untouchability and women's right to an equal share in inheritance. The state's record of giving legal protection to civil society is not bad, but civic norms have proved a teasing challenge. And it is not just ordinary people who violate them. Leaders of political parties don't ask why the road was dug to erect welcome gates for their brief visit. Police jeeps don't follow traffic rules, so why should owners of Dobermanns mind unleashing them in parks? A holistic view is a must for controlling one's anger in each one of these and dozens of similar situations. The law passed in Goa is a fine step to round off a century full of civic challenges.

On second thoughts, I imagined myself in Goa, and that I had spotted a man spitting on the street. What if I tried to get him caught? A dull pantomime of police and court procedures passed through my mind. I realized that it would be very hard to prove that the man I had seen spitting was indeed the same man. Being a lawyer's son, I have known since childhood what it means to gather a legally admissible proof. The difficulty of proving has to do with the suspicion everyone has of everyone else. Even the judges know that they are likely to be suspected if they apply judgement. That is why the benefit of doubt is given so generously. Why wouldn't it be available to the man who merely spat on a road? He could easily argue that I had mistaken him for someone else, and his lawyer would easily prove that by establishing how bad my eyesight is. That means I would have to organize a witness, preferably a policeman, before framing someone.

This little unpleasant reverie brought me back to my own world of school textbooks and teachers, who forthrightly forbid children to spit; and also explain why it is such a bad thing to do in public. They cover spitting as a sub-topic under respiratory ailments, which is in itself a sub-topic under common diseases. School texts and teachers discuss spitting the same way they discuss the five causes that triggered the revolt of 1857 and the six that account for its failure. All knowledge acquired at school has one major use—it helps you to get through the examination. The knowledge that spitting is bad for public health is no different. It has the added disadvantage that it tries to make you feel anxious about the unknown others.

If spitting were as harmful for the spitter as it is for those who happen to be around him or who walk a few steps behind him, then there might be chances for the caution against spitting to stick. Spitting clearly belongs to the category of activities like throwing garbage or playing loud music. You feel fine doing these things; it is someone else who suffers. To put oneself in the place of that someone calls for imagination, and as far as I know, imagination is no one's priority in education. I have read tomes on why India needs literacy, birth control, and computers, but I have never come across a word in favour of imagination.

That explains it! When a man spits, he spits on the strength of the illusion that he will not suffer the consequences. When spitting becomes habit, you stop noticing other spitters as potential sources of risk for your well-being. The risk is usually quite small, unless the diffuse grimness of something like the plague magnifies it. The sticky gob of spit that attaches to the sole of a Reebok is truly insignificant. Most probably, it will rub off or dry up when it comes in contact with dust or dry grass. The risk it poses to your health is much smaller than that posed by the thousands of tiny droplets floating in the air after the gob has fallen on earth.

In any case, many of us have the good habit of leaving our street shoes outside before entering the home, so the home and the world remain sharply distinguished as far as the sphere of risk from spitting is concerned. Nowhere else have I seen this distinction as sharply as in Patna. There, when you step into the street, you can see you are going to be in the middle of an ocean. The Matiz standing a few metres away becomes a little ship, shining above the waves of garbage. In the moment of opening the door, you are overwhelmed by the instinct to spit. If you are not a habitual spitter, you can identify the feelings mixed up in that instinct. Helplessness accounts for the biggest proportion; others are disgust at the amount of garbage you see, a sense of joy over the power you have to leave it behind, and the relief that you are about to exercise that power.

Possibly a good deal of spitting is accompanied by such feelings. Spitting on account of respiratory problems is different, though it is just as noisy and quite as regular as the more common form of spitting. Far too many people—and they are not all ageing—cough all the time, and coughing does compel them to spit every now and then. To that genre I have reconciled myself, for I know it is part of the air, and not just Delhi's air. They have sold Delhi's smoke-belching clunkers to smaller, unfortunate towns. I saw some of these buses in Jhansi recently and wondered how much more spitting the bus stand there can take. Maybe Delhi has a wee bit less of that kind of spitting. Nonetheless, it is in the less compelling forms of spitting that we can explore the depths of public psychology. Casual spitting has a distinct, voluntary character to it; at times we can guess that the guy was looking for something to do, or that he wanted to feel effective.

The sight/stench of garbage inevitably elicits spitting as a response from many people; but entirely private forms of dissatisfaction can have a similar effect. I have seen young male students spitting in the corridors of their own institution. Half an hour after getting a scolding or a bad mark, a girl might cry or sulk and the boy could well spit. And this difference between the sexes continues into adulthood. I rarely see women spitting in public; the ones whom I asked why they don't said it would be terribly awkward to do so. Men, apparently, don't think so, or else they don't mind being awkward. In a scene drawn by the Hindi novelist Rajendra Yadav, throwing one's spit at the greatest possible distance becomes a matter of contest among adolescent boys. The scene suggests the usual male urge to reach out farthest, which implies that spitting in public is yet another form that sexual frustration takes from boyhood onwards. This kind of pop psychology promises far too much, but let us not deny ourselves the hope that with more boys and girls studying together, this particular source of the frequent urge to spit will diminish.

Other causes will remain. The most obvious one is the lack of a discouraging ethos. Indians who go and live abroad stop spitting on streets virtually the day that they land in this 'other' country. What transforms them so magically is the absence of other spitters. The aggressively tidy condition of the roads and sidewalks also acts as a deterrent. It is not just spitting, but littering too that must stop before our streets can look tidy. Spitting is not just spitting: it conveys our generalized indifference to the job of keeping things clean, to the men and women who do that job for a living. There are people who spit at the sight of a sweeper.

The salaries paid to sweepers by wealthy house owners and municipal authorities is a form of spitting too. It is hardly a co-incidence that the job of sweeping absorbs the highest number of employed Scheduled Caste men and women, for whom a reservation exists in every other public job. The reservation policy has made some difference to the chances of a Scheduled Caste boy or girl securing a white-collar job, but it has done little to weaken the caste system that denies dignity to the job of removing garbage. The caste system poses a tough hurdle for India's brave campaign to establish individual dignity and social justice as civic and political values. At his last lecture in Delhi, our greatest expert on caste, the late M.N. Srinivas, sounded dismayed by the politics of caste; but he remained hopeful that as a concept, caste was giving way. To the extent Srinivas was right, we can hope that a few decades from now we will not hear that intermittent roar of spitters during a morning walk in a garden or while having breakfast in a train.

Much will depend on the state's ability to introspect and relate to people. The state, after all, has been our main instrument of social change. Its record of law-making is good, but its sincerity is permanently under the stress of circumstances it creates for itself. Last spring, the Delhi government suddenly announced an instant fine of Rs 50 for anyone found littering. Mobile courts with temporarily hired magistrates—ex-servicemen were pressed into service—created a minor scare. Some of my students took it seriously. A fortnight later, when President Clinton's visit had passed, life returned to normal.

The plague was similar. The few weeks its scare lasted, civic authorities seemed full of energy and resolve. DDT, gamaxin powder, and the smiling face of Gandhi were everywhere. The plague had taught a lesson, one thought. Then it passed, silently; a couple of scientists claimed it was proxy-plague, not the real thing. Municipal officers returned to their seats and the streets were back under spitters and sweepers. Six years on, I remember the plague as a festival of fear, when old instincts fell unconscious, and new ones wondered if their time had come. All festivals have that kind of effect. Even Patna looks stunningly tidy six days after Diwali, on Chhath. Nobody spits, no one litters, no one speaks unkindly to women. Bihari friends tell me it all happens without official help. Patna looks beautiful on that day.

2

Teaching Peace

As you mellow, the urge to compromise hits oftener, but latecomers continue to annoy me. During my long teaching career, I have tried many different ways to reform the unpunctual. My methods have been effectively challenged by the articulate, who used my pedagogy of connecting classroom learning with life outside to argue that Delhi buses and distances had made punctuality unsustainable as a daily value. Between secret appreciation of such facetious points and continued annoyance, I have usually chosen the latter, but this option did not seem right for my peace education course which had its dry run three years ago. How can a peace class start with anger? Fortunately, the first batch of seventeen had no persistent latecomers. In the second batch, however, I faced three.

One day when we were to start a fresh topic I waited for all three for about ten minutes. One of them came in at this point but the other two were still in a bus as I could imagine. The topic was human relations with nature. I had planned a silent reading from a book about Japanese gardens and a discussion thereafter, focusing on the role that *everything*, even stones and mud, plays in shaping our experience of a Japanese garden. I did not want the two remaining unpunctuals to miss the start, but I was getting anxious that if we waited any longer no one might have sufficient time to read in silence without stress. My additional anxiety was about the discussion afterwards. Having spent two decades at India's premier teacher training institute, I had compromised willy-nilly with the idea of a planned lesson. This morning I was determined to follow the plan I had drawn up for the direction in which I wanted the discussion to go. How would I carry out this plan properly now, with thirteen minutes already gone, waiting for my last two challengers? How much easier would it be if I could assume that they were not coming that day, due to sudden illness which is so common in Delhi. My trouble was that I knew from experience that these two students are not capable of getting sick. They were simply late, as always, and would show up, eventually, testing my patience, consideration, and compassion—the fundamental qualities our course on peace education, as approved by the Academic Council, loudly announced as being basic to peace.

At the start of the sixteenth minute, when I had finally decided to distribute the write-up on Japanese gardens—though I somehow knew my planned discussion was heading towards unseemly collapse—my dear ones arrived. Their characteristic knock at the door aroused that sudden flame of anger no training can control. Even before I could fight my desire to ignore their knock, I could picture the two of them feeling embarrassed, adjusting their gaze so it wouldn't have to face mine, trying to walk past a giggling class which was all too familiar with this daily drama. Over the next minute or so, this expected drama unfolded, with the addition of sounds produced by chairs being dragged and adjusted and dusted because the seating pattern had been seriously disturbed on account of an upheaval in our room and the rest of our institute's building, caused by repairs designed as part of the heritage restoration in the university campus. The two young women had to sit right at the back, in the middle of a jungle of mixed furniture brought from the adjoining room where heritage works—read demolition, to begin with—had begun.

Just as I was beginning to distribute the Japanese garden reading, I noticed we had thirty minutes left for this period. Something broke inside me, and something else took birth. What came up in a surge of anger was the passionate urge to get to the bottom of my failure to induce universal punctuality in my little class after three decades of being a teacher, two as a teacher of would-be teachers. Things cannot go on like this, I heard myself saying; let us find out why the late come so late.

The usual arguments and examples started pouring in. Someone said it is a matter of individual choice. Someone else said it depends on how seriously you take your studies. Do you all agree, I asked the rest, some of them wondering whether I had abandoned the day's topic. Does everyone agree that this is a matter of choice as Asmita says, I repeated, referring to the girl who had made the point. After a moment of silence in which we heard a sparrow from the back window, Sneha—one of the latecomers—said, 'Sir, Asmita lives in the hostel.' Nearly everybody laughed. Expectedly angry, Asmita said, 'Sir has forbidden personal factors as a basis for argument. I know that punctuality is a matter of preference.' Silence prevailed once more. Her logic was impeccable. It made me realize how pointless it was to look for reasons for unpunctuality without allowing personal factors to be taken into account. The reason why I had decided to ban them a month ago was because the course demanded meditation on collective responsibility, which seemed incompatible with personal complaints over a group assignment failing to materialize on time. Now I realized that some personal information might be worth sharing; perhaps it would help if those who came from long distances and still arrived on time discussed how they managed their morning routines. It would inspire the three chronic cases, I thought.

It was a new start, and I am not sure whether everybody saw it in a positive light. Some, who routinely arrived early, were visibly disappointed as they wondered if there was going to be no real teaching, that is, teaching on the topic of that day. They too, however, joined in cheerfully when the new topic opened up. We all felt a little bewildered, as students, whose faces we were all familiar with, told us things about their homes and routines, some of which were remarkably inconvenient or even painfully bizarre. For instance, we learned that one of the few male students in the class cooked for his sister who had a much tougher life than his. Vasudha, who seldom spoke on her own during discussions, described the great number of things she did for her chronically sick mother before coming to the class. A number of class members acquired a new image and respect, but the three unpunctuals had nothing much to offer which might inspire us to view their annoying habit with greater tolerance. All they could mention were long distances and difficult bus routes, requiring change and waiting.

We were nearly finished with listening to everybody's morning life when a myna came in, sat on the ceiling fan and started chattering loudly as only mynas can, without provocation. On earlier days, we had dealt with pigeons and sparrows, but the myna seemed more self-confident. Asmita looked at her and said, 'Sir, she too wants to talk about her morning routine!' This was a fine statement coming from Asmita who was feeling a little inane since she had no special morning narrative to offer as a hosteller. Her remark cheered her up and everybody else too. It gave me an interesting idea which vaguely reflected the topic we had fully abandoned. I asked, 'From how far do you think this myna has come?' No one took this question seriously, but it propelled me to go a step further, 'What else is present in our class that might have come from afar?' It was obvious that I was now referring to non-human participants, but were they living or non-living? This question came from Rekha, one of the habitual latecomers. 'Never mind,' I said, 'say whatever you notice'. She thought for a long second and then surprised everybody by saying that the electricity giving our tube lights their energy had come from God knows where. Two students immediately intervened, 'You know it is coming from Indraprastha Estate.' This is the name of Delhi's notorious thermal power station. 'How do you know for sure?' Rekha asked. 'It might be coming from the national grid—it is all connected, you know.' There was silence. Even the myna turned quiet. My job in such moments comes down to prompting further, so I said, 'That's a great thought. Let us see if there are any other long-distance participants in our class.'

The matter had so fully opened up by now that it required no additional prompting. My students started spotting things at a wild, inspired speed. Dust on the desks! The air! The sounds of traffic! One by one they quickly exhausted the potential of this exotic exercise. The dust seemed to have travelled the longest distance indeed—from Rajasthan as everybody thought. I was ready to conclude, 'So, is that the longest commuter?' We were uncertain, a little non-serious too, but still not quite ready to let the quiz die. Everyone thought hard for half a minute, and then Jyoti noticed the long patch of sun as it lay across the floor. She said, 'It's not the dust. The sun has travelled lakhs of miles.' I was stunned. So was everyone else. We had become aware of a phenomenon we had never thought about, how the sun came from so far away to make our class happen. The pedagogue in me could hardly resist using Jyoti's insight to teach Rekha a lesson. 'How does the sun manage to come on time despite its long journey?' To my utter surprise, she took it well, thought for a second, and then replied, 'You are right, Sir, but the sun doesn't change buses!'

The bell rang. As its authoritarian sound came pouring in, I felt we had learnt the topic of the day without using the reading I had selected. It would still help, I thought, and distributed the three-page essay about Japanese gardens. As I personally gave everyone a copy, I said it would strengthen what we had discussed that day. There was no need to bring it back unless they had questions, I told the class. 'What about attendance?' several students asked as they always did. 'It wouldn't be accurate,' I said, 'because the myna has already left.' The students laughed as they started leaving. Did that lesson, unplanned as it turned out, achieve anything? Behaviourist readers of this article have every right to ask: did the three habitual latecomers improve? Yes, they did, I am happy to recall, but the course could not continue for long for reasons out of my control, so I cannot say if the bad habit changed for good. From the perspective which evolved that morning, it hardly matters because the class changed annoyance into insight, a much higher goal than punctuality. We also came to know each other's lives better, and developed a sense of community. A miracle had occurred, without an effort or plan, which is characteristic of miracles. The unpredicted outcomes of learning are far more important than the ones we can predict and plan for. This is so because the crisis caused by violence and conflicts in the human world is far deeper and more vast than any rational plan can resolve. Only miracles can, if we let them happen, as they do quite often, without coming across as noticeable events.

* * *

The episode described above has incarnated in many forms among the students comprising the five batches that have so far opted for my peace education course. As a frequent problem, unpunctuality has been well matched by absenteeism. The Indian system allows students to miss one-fourth of the total number of classes held for any subject, but that is not the only reason why students absent themselves now and then. The crowd of activities and assignments they are surrounded by in the customary annual routine of a teacher training programme cause their own fatigue and encourage even the more devoted to strategize. In my peace education class, I have tried to take up this reality as a collective problem. While discussing the Dalai Lama's idea of universal responsibility, we wondered how the absent affect those present in the class. The fact they cannot contribute to the discussion without being present is bad enough; worse is the burden they put on the next class, by sounding unprepared or by asking inane questions. Even the least enthusiastic students understood this point when they heard someone who had been absent for two or three consecutive classes explaining his or her case. 'Why did you do that? What was the compulsion?' Such questions sometimes elicited an answer referring to sickness, and fellow students reluctantly accepted this kind of answer. One or two asked the absentee to look at personal health as a common, public issue. But when the absentee mentioned a marriage in the family or an extended religious ritual as the reason of absence, most of the class registered a sense of outrage. In the most recent batch, the entire class decided that they will implement Gandhi's recommendation for guilt-arousal as a means to improve regularity. I have not seen a better example of a peace strategy in action, both to appreciate the subtle presence and meaning of conflict and the possibility of mitigating it without the use of coercion. Peace education can hardly afford to become yet another area of knowledge in which students learn in order to be examined.

3

Freire's Legacy

Paulo Freire's death in the summer of 1997 remained largely unnoticed in India's academic world. That makes sense, considering how marginal a presence education has as an area of enquiry in our academia. What makes things worse for Freire's memory is the strange fact that in India the Left, unlike the Right, has no serious concern for education. But even the world of non-governmental organizations (NGOs), which owes a substantial part of its current key vocabulary and its legitimacy to Freire, paid him no major tribute. To an extent we can attribute this indifference to the general despair prevailing among those who believe that ideas ought to permeate social action. A possible parallel reason relates to the culture of activism that treats any time taken for reflection, for example, reflection on a departee's legacy, as an essentially academic exercise, implying second-rate importance. The concept of activism is a part of Freire's legacy, and though an incomplete part, it often connotes the only form of resistance that has the potential to work. Finally, one other reason for the indifference shown to Freire may be the steady decline of Freire's own distinctiveness over the last few years of his life. Freire's rise as a source of dramatic influence, and an eventual 'fall' constitute a story of historical value, especially from the viewpoint of colonized societies like India.

Towards the end of the 1960s, Freire was thrown into exile by the military rulers of his native Brazil. They had found the 43-year old Freire guilty of encouraging peasants to reflect on their own condition with a view to waging a collective effort towards changing it. For Freire, this was an educational engagement with the people. Out of this experience and the response it received from the people and their military rulers, Freire composed his elaborate philosophical statement which first appeared in English translation in the early 1970s under the title *Pedagogy of the Oppressed*.[1] Within a short while, the book became a worldwide hit, initially competing with another popular text of the 1970s, namely *Deschooling Society*[2] by Ivan Illich, but eventually outpacing it. Illich himself described Freire's book as 'a truly revolutionary pedagogy'. Several other books by Freire followed, but for the vast majority of his readers *Pedagogy* remained his most reliable and distinctive statement. Freire resented this fact as any writer would, but he acknowledged his readers' identification of him with his first book by naming his penultimate book as *Pedagogy of Hope*.[2] Published in 1994, it provides a collection of personal narratives on the reception of the first *Pedagogy*. Freire's last book, published just before his death, was *Letters to Cristina*,[3] his niece to whom he wrote some eighteen long letters explaining his life and work. The last letter shows how anxious Freire was in the evening of his life about the threat posed to human dignity and freedom by what he called the rebirth of Nazi-Fascist ideology everywhere and the Left's vacillating stance towards its own role.

The climate of ideas which characterized the early 1970s greatly explains the popularity of Freire's *Pedagogy of the Oppressed*. Hope for the downtrodden had been running high since the late 1960s, riding the tide of anti-Vietnam war

---

[1] Continuum, New York, 1970.
[2] Continuum, New York, 1997.
[3] Routledge, New York, 1968.

feelings in the United States and the sweeping successes of Mao's Red Guards in China. The crude attempt made by the Soviet Union to maintain its dominance in Eastern Europe helped only to underline the importance of people in relation to governments. Student protests against university curricula in France and elsewhere had called into question the old, established structures of knowledge. The turn of the decade offered a remarkably fertile climate to sociologists and other analysts of educational systems. They marshalled a strong case for suspecting the role of education in the context of constructing a civil society by purely constitutional means. Uncovering the hidden, and later on not-so-hidden, agenda of hegemonic elements active in shaping education became the central preoccupation of educational research and rendered an impressive yield of studies and ideas. Freire's *Pedagogy* came as a kind of last word in this ethos, its uniqueness residing in the fact that it presented not just an erudite analysis of the evil that schools perpetrate, but also an exciting remedy.

Freire's major contribution to progressive educational theory lay in his attempt to introduce 'oppression' as a basic variable in the model of human society that education had to deal with. Oppression, we can say, is the connecting theme of all his works. Freire suggests that any educational theory which does not deal with the problem of oppression is incomplete and unacceptable. The humanistic agenda of education has no meaning or validity, we feel while reading Freire's writings, if educators and the curriculum they uphold ignore the decline of humanity into an oppressor–oppressed duality. He argues that prevailing educational practices by and large exacerbate the dehumanized state of the human world. This critique, as well as the remedy of 'cultural action' that he offers, present at least as intellectually rich, if not as comprehensive, a model of education as Dewey had presented at the beginning of the century. Freire's model is more promising, at least to an Indian eye, than Dewey's in the present run of things, simply because it acknowledges conflict, and that too the specific conflict arising from colonial subjugation as the primary backdrop for making sense of the present-day world. As Freire explained to his niece, 'while the centre of power, the north has become accustomed to framing the south, the north "gives a north" to the south.' Education is not worthy of being called education, we learn from Freire, if its epistemology does not reflect a critical perspective on injustice and oppression. In Freire's highly normative concept of education, learning necessarily implies an awareness of how 'my' condition is related to the state of the world. And such awareness must meet the other standard set by Freire: the motivation to make one's contribution to some form of collective action.

The focus of pedagogic effort, in Freire's model, is on the cultural dimension of oppression. Although he sees oppression both in economic or material and cultural terms, it is in the cultural domain that he finds the key role of education. All his books emphasize the need for analysing culture as a means to identify the implications of oppression for the human personality and the social order. In this choice of culture as a critical area for education, he follows the established tradition of Marxist scholarship on Latin America and African history, especially on colonization, and the socialist streak in theological literature. In Freire's approach to literacy, 'cultural action' is aimed at setting the learner free to apply reason. 'Conscientizing' involves an awareness that the oppressed are the creators of culture, and that the oppressors have, for generations, dispossessed them not only of the products of culture but also of the awareness that they are the true or authentic representatives of culture. In Freirean methodology, a literacy class is to be treated as a 'culture circle' where the relationship of men and women with nature is to be 'read' by reflecting on the work they do on natural material, such as clay (that is, while making a vase for sale), in order to transform such material into a resource for learning. This kind of 'reading' of the world, its past and present, must precede, and not follow, the ability to read the word. For example, an illustration given in

Education for Critical Consciousness[4] presents the sketch of a vase with flowers as a point of discussion on the theme of human relations with nature. Freire's commentary says: 'During a discussion of this situation in a Culture Circle of Racife, I was moved to hear a woman say with emotion, 'I make culture. I know how to make that (the vase).'

In all the situations illustrated in this manner in *Education for Critical Consciousness,* the emphasis is on digging out and revealing the original, that is prehistoric and historical, layers of the working men and women's consciousness of their role and importance. There is a distinct Jungian feel to the whole exercise. The illustrations given are stark, suggesting a kind of palaeography of the mind. It is important to note that all these 'situations' proposed for pre-literacy discussion portray pre-industrial or non-industrial kinds of work, such as hunting, digging a well, and pottery. The only symbol of technological advancement included among these generative themes, as they were to be called, is a rifle, used by a 'lettered hunter'. Members of the culture circle are expected to discuss how the technological progress symbolized by the rifle represents 'man's increasing opportunity' which has meaning 'only to the extent that it contributes to the humanisation of man, and is employed towards his liberation'.

In this important early work we can recognize the 'fundamentalist' aspect of Freire which was ignored in a determined manner by countless agencies of adult or community education and governments in all kinds of countries. There was something rugged about Freire's philosophy and programme. It was clearly a utopian programme, but encased in its transformative vision was space for dialogue with dissenters. Although boldly prescriptive, and in that sense incompatible with the usual style of liberal pedagogues, especially in adult education, Freire's pedagogic stance seemed to question the state's monopoly over defining the post-World War II visions of modernization

[4] Seabury Press, New York, 1973.

and development. Though there was no straight reference to industrialization or any elaborate discussion of it in his writings, an implied criticism of industrialized man and that of the structures under which men and women were forced to live by conditions of industrialization was all too evident. This implied criticism had many resonances; the ones of Marx and the Frankfurt school were easy to hear, but deeper down the voice of a Christian theologian reflecting on the poor—the ones actively dispossessed in the course of the worldwide hunt for resources, labour, and markets—could also be heard. Freire's historical perspective strongly reminded one of the dependency school of Latin American social scientists, such as Andre Gunder Frank and Paul Boran. His educational principles were pervasive, inviting us to view educational change as a generalized process of the structural adjustment of a world constructed by colonialism. The point was made amply clear in *Pedagogy in Process*,[5] a collection of letters from Guinea Bissau: 'to discuss education, I repeat, is to think of the overall plan for the society itself.'

Freire's method compels us to reflect on education in the context of a generalized critique of the organization of society, its process of production, its systems of communication, and the values practised in its attempt to survive or prevail. That means the task of making people literate includes the exploration of all salient features of social life, such as institutions of race and caste, ownership of natural resources, and the patterns of the consumption of these resources. Such an exploration is not a 'post-literacy', but rather a 'pre-literacy' exercise. If this exercise is regarded as an essential part of Freire's method, then we can appreciate why it has no real use for the expert or bureaucrat who only wants to improve teaching techniques or material. Yet, despite being of little use to such people, the vocabulary associated with Freire's method proved greatly attractive to them. In country after country, including our

[5] *The Letters to Guinea Bissau*, Seabury Press, New York, 1978.

own, it was co-opted by official programmes of mass literacy, with the obvious objective of imparting to these programmes a progressive gloss that might conceal their coercive character. These programmes were designed to socialize the masses into accepting the prevailing oppressive order as the only order, rudimentary literacy acting as a means to expose them more fully to the prevailing order so as to articulate and reinforce their acceptance of it.

In a theoretical sense, Freire's mode of 'deep literacy' had a refreshing feel to it because it offered an intrinsic critique of, as well as an alternative to, the well-established behaviourist model of literacy. As a theory of learning, behaviourism has continued to dominate educational practice, including teacher education. Its appeal is rooted in its positivistic methodology and its promise of making the outcomes of teaching predictable. By insisting on a minimalist approach to outcomes and on explicitly made responses, behaviourism trivializes the concept of learning. The concept of learning intrinsic to behaviourism, resonated the temptation—felt in every country in varying degrees—to use mass education as a means of socializing the younger generation, to shape its basic need structure and loyalties, in accordance with the ideology and lifestyle of dominant groups. Both nationalism and capitalism heightened this temptation. In countries of the West and the colonized Third World, these two forces often worked together to determine the goals of mass education. In the communist world, the temptation to consolidate the nation-state by the ideological use of mass education required no justification or cover.

Freire struck at the behaviourist underpinnings of mass education in a manner one would least expect to succeed. The list of ten characteristics of 'banking education' given in *Pedagogy* were highly simplistic and decontextualized too—indeed the whole book was. Many such listings had been done earlier by liberal critics of schooling. What was special about Freire's listing was that he used it as the ground on which a link between behaviourist pedagogy and the oppressive and unjust global order could be established: Freire avoided a frontal attack on the forces inimical to humanist education by not naming them, and we can guess why. Naming them would have limited his appeal to specific audiences steeped in similar naming. For instance, by naming capitalism as the core of the de-humanizing system of education, he would have run the risk of being seen as yet another Marxist critic of capitalism. Both he and Illich, who also mounted a strong critique of mass schooling in the 1970s, avoided such clubbing by leaving their readers free to wonder about their intellectual slants. It would be correct to say that neither Freire nor Illich had ideological loyalties. They were both radical preachers, though Illich had been officially questioned and forced out of a formal affiliation to the Catholic Church after an elaborate quarrel which he elaborately documented. Freire expanded his role as a preacher by assembling an all-out attack on a world characterized by gross material inequalities and cultural subordination. Freire's writings leave us in no doubt that the unjust order in which humanity is stuck cannot be challenged by developmentalist measures. He emphasizes the unavoidable necessity of a revolution, but the nature of the revolution remains unclear, except that it must be based on an existential dialogue between those who attempt to mobilize others and these others. Freire's discussion of a revolutionary strategy is full of echoes; different kinds of readers can read the philosophers of their choice into Freire's words.

So it is not surprising, though it is disappointing to those who expected Freire's influence to extend policy options in post-colonial societies, that his books were reinvented in all manners even as the crisis of the post-war international order deepened. During the decades when Freire became an inevitable reference in writings and courses on socially purposive education, oppression became a generalized state of being, of which just about everyone could partake, depending on the aspect from which representation of the self was required on a given occasion. In the background of this fluidity was the decline of objectivity as a means of knowing, and the blurring of categories which promised to distinguish one kind of existence and perspective from another. Freire had defined objectivity as a characteristic of knowledge about people which included their own awareness of their situation. He had hoped to push educational planning beyond its typical database assembled with the help of a normative survey. His concern with the fuller situational picture, of which people's daily life was a part, implied that those who organize literacy programmes and other such activities will stop decontextualizing people, stereotyping them as a part of a process which ultimately aims at disbursing prefabricated solutions to problems. But Freire's programme of developing in the planner and the teacher a certain degree of sensitivity to people's own perspective, and not just their suffering, assumed an ethical commitment to social transformation. This quality became increasingly scarce with the rise of developmentalism as a global financial enterprise. Aid from the rich nations to the poor had been used as a political tool earlier, but during the 1980s it became a specific instrument of quelling the social unrest anticipated in the wake of a neo-imperialist onslaught of the regime of capital, accompanied by the expansion of satellite communication and transmission technologies.

The collapse of the Soviet Union and its empire, and the fresh impetus with which corporate interests struck out for markets and resources, together altered the nature and logic of social action in the 1990s. The establishment of communication links on a larger scale than ever before radically enhanced the reach of financial capital. A general sense of despair and puzzlement set in among Left-leaning scholars and leaders of social action who were not necessarily admirers of the Soviet model. China's warm overtures towards absorbing Western capital gave further sharpness to the feeling that the world was destined to become even more like what it had been, at least in the near future. The only revolution, this feeling suggested, that one might talk about with certainty was going to be in technology, especially that of communication and manipulation of information. For the political economy of poorer countries, the most important changes were going to be in factors of trade. The emerging world scenario seemed to strengthen the hold of the rich on natural resources and markets everywhere. In politics, the memory of the anti-colonial struggle was getting increasingly confused with the claims of neo-fascist elements that they alone represented cultural and political autonomy. Liberal spaces, where occasional resistance and critical enquiry might flourish, had started to close in even as the loud cacophony of personal consumption had become the main content of every media of information. Activism aimed at social change had become a service industry, generously funded by international donors with a clear view that it would help contain within limits the feelings of the poor and the marginalized majority.

This portrait of the past decade or so, though sketchy, should help us appreciate the incorporation of Freirean ideas and terminology into the industry of voluntarism. The decline of state interest, formally, as a condition of structural adjustment in improving public education and health pushed voluntary activism towards centre stage. Public debate on state policy and efficiency shrunk. Social-scientific endeavour to make sense of things started to look irrelevant, and job opportunities for young social researchers got confined to mechanized services and temporary involvements. The social science disciplines were also facing an internal crisis, brought about by the questions inherent in certain postmodern literary theorists concerning the stability and reliability of meaning in texts, including scholarly texts which provide historical and sociological analysis. Part of a broader postmodern front which promised to free the European mind from the memory of colonization and the Nazi holocaust, such questioning gained easy currency in the Indian academia, chronically starved as it is of opportunities to contribute to theory-building. The new textualists emphasized the authenticity of experience, suggesting that no one could speak on behalf of others, hence any attempt to give a voice to the less articulate was at best meaningless, and at worst a patronizing act worthy of suspicion.

The concept of education as a voice-giving activity was inherent in Freire's association between illiteracy and what he called the 'culture of silence'. His insistence on historical analysis of the conditions in which the masses were living added perhaps an unbearable burden on prevailing conceptions of social work, but the basic premise that an educative activity involves external intervention was a part of his model too. For Freire, successful education should present a new situation, not merely a sharpened version of people's common sense. The argument put forward by certain postmodernists that all representations are merely narratives, hence the need to accept infinite relativism, constituted a direct threat to the validity of Freire's model. His rebuttal of non-interventionism comes in a dialogue published in the *Harvard Educational Review*[6] and we hardly need to be surprised by its unequivocal tone:

I think it is an ethical duty for educators to intervene in challenging students to critically engage with their world so they can act upon it and on it. I do not accept the present philosophical posture in which truth is relative and lies and truths are merely narratives. They have the right to say so. They also have the right to say, as some thinkers have been saying, that with the fall of communism we have reached the end of history. They have all the right to propose what they want to propose, as I also have the right to reject their proposals. I would have to point out that history continues, and I cannot remain silent before an error. By the same token, if a student wants to kill himself in front of me in my class, I cannot remain neutral: I must intervene, as I must intervene in teaching the peasants that their hunger is socially constructed and work with them to help identify

[6] Paulo Freire and Donaldo P. Macedo, 'A Dialogue: Culture, Language, and Race', Fall 1995, pp. 377–402.

those responsible for this social construction, which is, in my view, a crime against humanity.[7]

This elaborate explanation, and especially its justificatory tone, shows how afflicted Freire was by the philosophy of non-interventionism and its implications for educational theory.

His legacy needs to be assessed in the context of the crisis in which educational theory finds itself. In the Third World, the locus of Freire's theory, there seems to be no end in sight to the sharp contradiction between the two primary functions of education, namely, its selective or certifying function, and its function in enhancing the intellectual capital of society. The predominance of the first function is so overwhelming that the latter gets no chance to receive attention. As a consequence of this self-perpetuating situation, what Freire had called 'banking education' is flourishing. 'Banking education' is likely to flourish even more vigorously in the years to come as a result of the further consolidation of class conflict in the wake of the globalization of exploitation and consumption. Trivialization of knowledge and intellectual capacity, as one of the many outcomes of the speed-centred technologies of transmission and retrieval of information, can also be expected to fortify 'banking education'. These technologies pose a more general challenge to educational theory, applicable to the wealthy world as well, which arises from the diminution of space or milieu as a factor in learning. Engagement with the immediate milieu, both natural and social, which Dewey had proposed as one of the foundations of progressive education, has run into deep trouble with the advent of the online lifestyle as a symbol of status and power. Even before the advent of this kind of space-conquering oblivion as a symbol of status and power, indifference to the costs of capitalist opulence of the West incurred by the world's poor had become an acceptable feature of the Western-educated

---

[7] 'Cultural Action for Freedom', *Harvard Educational Review*, May and August 1970.

man and woman's personality. Throughout the 1980s one could notice the increase of inward-looking tendencies even among critical, Left-leaning scholars. Their willingness to accept a 'coping' stance in the face of mounting pressures on the social foundations of educational theory was all too obvious. The challenge proposed by Rousseau, namely, to nurture the citizen without stifling the human, was becoming increasingly elusive as a goal of public education in the Western world, against a background of sweeping strides made by neo-imperialist ideologies.

Can we then say that Freire provided a mere ideological sop to live by during a period of all-round gloom and difficulties for humanist education? It is hardly unfair to say that Freire belongs to that short historical period which lasted from the late 1960s to the mid-1980s. Unmasking the powers of the oppressor seemed strangely sufficient in this period. Freire too did not offer any guiding clues on what might come after people have been conscientized. In the case of quite a few efforts inspired by Freire's ideas, local success in breaking the culture of silence was received with quiet suppression of the conscientized poor by their powerful masters and the state. Many drew the conclusion that Freirean pedagogy needed a wider, organized political movement to sustain conscientization. This conclusion was consistent with the Left's customary approach to regard educational reorganiz-ation as a post-revolutionary activity.

Perhaps Freire intended, like Gramsci, to make political action against oppressive economic relations more democratic by permeating it with a definitive cultural stirring. In retrospect, it seems correct to say that Freire's emphasis on culture as the locus of educational effort was misinterpreted under the circumstances prevailing and unfolding in the 1980s. In India, the shedding of socio-cultural concerns by institutionalized politics gained speed from the early 1980s onwards. The Emergency was the watershed after which political activity became exclusively concerned with power games, and the broader politics of social change fell to the share of non-party activists. Freire had warned us about such a separation in his first book, by criticizing 'activism' as the obverse of 'verbalism', the former being devoid of reflection and the latter of action. This and many other philosophical insights are part of Freire's legacy, which we now have enough time to peruse as we can afford a fuller view of the pottery of the post-war international order. We should now know better that so-called globalization marks no change, and that there are no shortcuts to evolving a society in which peace is based on justice.

That Freire chose to title one of his two last books as *Pedagogy of Hope* is not without significance for guessing how he might have wanted his legacy to be read, at least in the immediate future. Defending hope as an 'ontological need', he cautions us in this book against optimism for its own sake as well as against the reduction of struggle to 'calculated acts' or to a 'purely scientific approach'. Increasingly more blatant strategies continue to surface to co-opt Freire into standardized, and almost inevitably internationally funded, global programmes of adult education. Funders and organizers of such programmes mouth the familiar vocabulary of dialogue, struggle, and empowerment, garnish this vocabulary with references to the promise of new communications technology and present a recipe for change in the destiny of the poor. To maintain Freire's holistic vision of social action in a world ridden with globally mobile resource persons and, by definition, uninvolved consultants, is difficult indeed. Even more difficult is to recall as a point of reference the subtle presence of Christian austerity in Freire's world of values. The application he found for Martin Buber's concept of 'dialogue', and the attempt he made to establish dialogue as an existential necessity and as a definitive means of producing knowledge will remain major theoretical contributions to education. How his idea of knowledge as a tacit product of dialogue can be nurtured and explored further in a world held together by electronic impulses and nuclear deterrence is a question that those interested in Freire's legacy must attend to in the years to come. For the passing moment, these words from his final letter to his niece have an eerie ring of relevance:

The fascist threat may grow to the extent that, overwhelmed, the Left vacillates between denying itself by believing in neo-liberal discourse... and reactivating Stalinism. Undeniably, the role of the Left today is to believe that it does exist, and to abandon authoritarianism and dogmatism. It is to overcome historical, philosophical, and epistemological errors, for example, that of setting socialism and democracy against each other.[8]

[8] *Letters to Cristina*, p. 188.

4

A Child's Swaraj

Had I not offered to write on the Pippi trilogy as my choice for the book of the millennium, and had I not been asked to confine myself to children's literature, I would have selected *Hind Swaraj*, which is just as nasty as the Pippi story. *Hind Swaraj* happens to be the only book we Indians are left with to recall what we expected from ourselves. Now that we have exploded atomic bombs of our own under the sands of Rajasthan, we look like anybody else. Gandhi, meanwhile, has been grabbed—though not quite so firmly yet—by post-Godse Gandhians. They look wonderfully happy thinking we have forgotten that Godse was one of them. Of course, they are perfectly justified, for there is nothing illegal in imagining that Gandhi's murder was a freak end of his freak personality and life, not the consequence of an ideological movement. In modern terms, morality has far less importance than legality. This change absolves Godse after his death by legal hanging and makes *Hind Swaraj* quite irrelevant to the present-day world. This is not the case of Pippi Longstocking though she is just as awkward and her story asks us to give civil society just as radical a shake as Gandhi's book does.

Like *Hindi Swaraj*, Astrid Lindgren's Pippi trilogy is a statement of freedom, except that in Pippi's case the statement is made in a child's terms. Apart from finding it more relevant, I feel happier choosing the Pippi story to write on because

Hind Swaraj depresses me by reminding me of a huge loss of opportunity we Indians have suffered by sidelining Gandhi as a guide. We have been much too prudent and timid, and we are getting more so these days. Even our nursery-age children have started preferring to be proper and trying to look normal like adults. In my reading, no book advocates the value of awkwardness more colourfully than the story of Pippi does. Generations worth of child-rearing norms will stand threatened if the Pippi trilogy becomes popular reading—after every Indian child has learnt how to read. I believe that the social foundations of moral indifference and inertia are buried in certain child-rearing norms.

The Pippi trilogy was first published in the mid-1940s. First came *Pippi Longstocking* in 1945. Then, a year later, *Pippi Goes Abroad* was published; and the third book, *Pippi in the South Seas*, appeared in 1948. Looking at these dates one might sense a relationship between the Pippi saga and the spirit of reconstruction that spread across the European world following the end of the Second World War. Such a connection is not altogether misplaced, for the popularity of Pippi does owe to the post-war climate. She came across as a reminder of the joyful wildness of ordinary childhood, something that the war-torn West must have found refreshing, even nostalgic. However, the birth of Pippi predates the end of the war, for the story of her varied deeds was first narrated by Astrid Lindgren in 1941 to her daughter, Karin, who was sick in bed and wanted to hear about Pippi Longstocking, a name she had conjured up.

Pippi is not so much a post-war child as a fictional essence of the venturesome ideas and practices witnessed in children's education during the inter-war years in Europe. One tends to recall names like Neill and Russell to characterize this period, but the ferment they signify was much deeper and quite diverse in its manifestation. It was a period of intense craving and a kind of *jehad* to reorganize education according to the needs of childhood.

Why the task was felt to be so urgent during this particular period is a question that lies buried deep in the socio-political history of Europe. It seems as if many people sensed a great calamity approaching, and they wanted to prevent it by radically reforming education, acting under the belief that education was a key factor determining social destiny. Armed with the exciting psychological theories of Freud and Adler, they tried, but failed to prevent the big disaster which came in the shape of the second global war. It was as depressing an end as anyone might have imagined to the endeavours of the inter-war years, and to the dreams of a grand educational reconstruction. It was an old dream, having started in the eighteenth century with Locke and Rousseau. As if the war and the mega-sin committed in Germany was not enough, the end came with Hiroshima and Nagasaki.

Pippi encapsulates the long dream of a renovated childhood that Europe saw for two centuries while its real children were toiling in factories, dying in wars, and facing the consequences of an unprecedented upheaval in family and social relationships brought about by industrialization. Pippi is a remarkable strip of that great dream because she herself is so unassuming. She is a wonder girl who takes it easy. She is not out to improve society; she merely wants to live in it as an independent child. Who can forget the second sentence of the first Pippi book? 'She was nine years old, and she lived all alone.' You expect an explanation, and you get it in the third sentence, with unwelcome clarity if you are reading the book as an adult: 'She had neither mother nor father, which was rather nice. . .' And here onwards unfolds a long episodic story which can only be read and enjoyed by children, nine or ten years old. Adults who try to read it must have some rationale, such as writing a thesis on children's literature, or else they will find it superficial and absurd, even dull. The Pippi story is not about childhood; it is written for children, and children alone, unlike certain classics that adults as well as children enjoy reading. If Pippi makes an impact on children, then the adults are not supposed to know it—until it is too late.

Why the Pippi trilogy has been so popular is easy to appreciate. Apart from the ease with which the daily life episodes in Pippi's unusual routine are narrated, there are the wit, the humour, and the presence of mind that flash through every page. These come across better in the Swedish original, for Lindgren has used many colloquialisms, which are rooted in Sweden's not-so-lost rural ways of behaving and which are not fully translatable. But far above these features of style, I think the Pippi books absorb child readers so fully because they respond so earthily to the common urge for power which children everywhere have but cannot fulfil during childhood.

Pippi has the physical prowess of an order that stretches credulity. She can lift a horse, handle thieves and policemen, outdo teachers and ringmasters—all in a 'so what?' manner. As Una Lundqvist has remarked in her exhaustive study of the Pippi phenomenon, Pippi is an inverted Alice. Unlike the polite, well-groomed Alice who visits a strange world, the coarse, mischievous Pippi stays in the ordinary world and gives it a rough shake. She has the strength it takes to do so, and she also has the other thing one needs to escape criticism and to live independently: gold. Initially one gets the impression that her father is dead, but later we hear that her father left her plenty of gold before he left to become a pirate in the South Seas. If anyone wants to read a message in this, it is rather simple. The adult world is organized around two values: physical power and money. If you want to ponder on that, seeing it as an embedded comment, well, that is nice; but the author of the Pippi story does not give the impression that the story was written to point this out, let alone to comment on it. Lindgren is too deep an author to write a story in order to drive home this kind of point.

There are many other sides to Pippi, which make it hard to classify her as a wonder girl. She is often melancholic and regretful. She easily concedes a mistake, and she worries about hurting others' feelings. She can backtrack, which is quite shocking when it happens in the course of a narrative supposedly moving forward. My favourite scene belongs to one such episode. It comes at the end of the second book when Pippi is about to leave with her father, making everybody extremely upset, particularly Annika and Tommy who are her neighbours and closest friends. The farewell scene is dismal with Annika and Tommy deeply sad and weeping. The inevitable moment of departure comes. The ship's gangway is pulled up. Suddenly Pippi makes up her mind to cancel her journey. No one can believe it, least of all her father, but there it is—Pippi is determined to stay back. She says she cannot face her friends feeling so sad. Finding an excuse to agree, her father says that she will have a more regular life if she stays back. Pippi agrees too, but puts it startlingly differently. This is how the dialogue goes:

'You're right as always, my daughter,' said Captain Longstocking. 'Course your life is more regular at Villekula Cottage, and I'm sure that's best for little children.'

'Exactly,' said Pippi, 'it's definitely best for little children to have a regular life, especially if they can regulate it themselves.'

Pippi's decision to cancel her journey surprises everyone and makes Tommy and Annika happy. However, the text says that 'Annika had cried so much that she could not stop immediately'. If I had to argue why Astrid Lindgren is a great, perhaps the greatest living writer for children, I would quote that last sentence to show how well she knows children.

If a publisher decides to bring out Lindgren's books in India, reprinting the English translations that already exist, and arranging fresh translations into Indian languages (Pippi was partially translated into Hindi by Chandragupta Vidyalankar three decades ago), then I would suggest that Pippi should be supplemented by Ronia. Pippi will give us a big, bold break from the drivel most children are served in the name of reading in schools. She will embolden the next generation of children to take political leaders, big officers, and the rich in their stride. She will also give our boys and girls the courage to stand up to teachers who beat and parents who want their progeny to become this or that. Pippi's presence will serve a deeper need as well. The next few decades are going to be a trying time. West or East, childhood and education are both in crisis, and the crisis can only deepen. Childhood will have to be reinvented after the euphoria over toys like the Internet and the moral indifference to the nuclear bomb have passed. Pippi will be a fine companion for these difficult years, and Ronia, Lindgren's later creation, will help us overcome our enmity with our nearest neighbour.

Written some forty years after Pippi was conceived, *Ronia, the Robber's Daughter* is a sombre book for a morally confused and endangered world. Ronia has neither power nor gold of her own, but she triumphs in the end by demolishing the silly wall of hatred between two clans. She can potentially inspire our grandchildren to solve our Pakistan problem when all the tired and retired diplomats who pretend trying to solve it these days are gone. Pippi and Ronia can help us, provided one condition is met: they are popularized in Pakistan too, and if our defence minister is to be believed that China is our enemy number one, then in China too.

5

Remembering Earthworms

Earthworms are described in the *Encyclopedia of Indian Natural History* as 'familiar inhabitants of every garden', which can be seen 'in great abundance during the rains when they become very active'. This is precisely how I remember earthworms, literally taking over the house and garden within days of the arrival of monsoon. Nothing of this sort happens anymore. I recently spent one whole rainy evening with an old school friend, reconstructing eco-life of the 1960s in our part of Madhya Pradesh. Not just earthworms, but frogs, toads, and several varieties of butterflies and insects have also vanished. Earlier, frogs used to drown the human voice in our town, with their loud and collective croaking. Their presence on the streets during July and August made walking and cycling very difficult. Now you don't see or hear them even if you leave the town and walk to a nearby village pond. Something traumatic has occurred in the ecosystem, decimating these poor creatures and changing the face of the rainy season. My friend and I tried to figure out the source of that trauma, and our suspicion fell on chemical fertilizers and pesticides, which have been used in abundance since the late 1960s all over our district. After all, our district, though educationally depressed, has been in the forefront of the Green Revolution since its start in the late 1960s.

But the situation cannot be very different in other parts of India where the use of chemical fertilizers and pesticides has become a cult. Few among the educated seem to realize that reckless use of these fertilizers reduces the land's natural fertility, especially its capacity to replenish its nutrients after each crop. Heavily fertilized land may produce increased amounts of crop in the short run, but the crop is of poorer nutritional quality, and each successive crop demands increased quantities of chemical fertilizers. Economically too, chemical fertilizers have proved unviable for small-scale farmers, leading a large number of them into chronic debt. Increased financial inputs explain why greater production has not brought about much change in the poverty of small-scale peasants who form the majority of our peasantry.

However, chemical fertilizers are so well entrenched in the general discourse of agricultural development that anyone criticizing them is quickly labelled as an anti-modernist. Those who see merit in the ideas propagated by the Japanese naturalist Masanobu Fukuoka (the author of *One Straw Revolution*)[1] are customarily described as eccentrics. Naturally, his sharp critique of modern agriculture and his proposal for search of alternatives do not form part of the knowledge that passes for learning in our schools and colleges, and which reaches out to millions of young students each year. The message conveyed to them in textbooks is loud and clear: namely, that chemical fertilizers and pesticides hold the key to increased agricultural production and, therefore, to national progress.

This being a common theme of school knowledge, I was surprised to find a grade seven science textbook acknowledging the problem posed by the use of chemical fertilizers. The text says that these chemicals are washed off by rainwater into ponds and rivers, and since they do not get decomposed by natural methods or by microbes, they 'get accumulated and pollute the water'. As is customary with school textbooks, this

[1] Rodale Press, Emmaus, Pennsylvania, 1978.

shocking statement is followed by no details or suggestions for observation or activity. The child is left to wonder what damage chemically-polluted water might do to the ecosystem, including human beings.

The learning of science that our schools and colleges ostensibly promote does not encourage young people to link things up, making sense of what they see around them with the help of what information their texts and teachers might provide. This failure explains why the teaching of science does not promote a scientific temper, characterized by a questioning spirit and the desire to seek personal verification of given knowledge. Considering how poorly equipped our schools and colleges are with laboratory facilities, we cannot expect to provide adequate experience of scientific work to children if we depend on laboratory-based experiments alone. Teaching children to observe natural phenomena in outdoor settings would be a far superior practice for us, as the late J.B.S. Haldane had proposed several decades ago. By remaining stuck to the stereotype image of science as knowledge gained under controlled conditions, we have failed to modernize school science.

Another symptom of the unscientific temper our schools promote is the denial of recognition to unconventional—which in some cases is really conventional—knowledge. There is just one accepted approach or answer to each problem; anyone who dares to call attention to an alternative approach invites contempt and failure in the examination.

The concept of first aid provides a striking example of this kind of orthodoxy. The child who might include *arnica* and *cantharis* in his list of first-aid items, in addition to the usual gear, can only bring ridicule upon himself because these items are not mentioned in the prescribed text. The medicines I have named are well-known homoeopathic remedies for common injuries and burns, but homoeopathic knowledge is taboo in schools. Similarly, ayurvedic, unani, and traditional folk remedies have no chance of appreciative mention in school literature, let alone application in the fundamentalist universe of school science. Examples of this problem can be found in several areas such as nutrition, disease-control, energy resources, and so on.

Concern for animal and vegetational life is frequently heard these days as a message in classrooms and annual-day functions. The message, however, does not get translated into activities sustained over any length of time. One reason is the dominance of a crude version of the concept of objectivity. The way this concept is applied in science teaching, it implies the refusal to associate any feelings with living natural phenomena. Children are, of course, told that cruelty to animals is bad, but the learning of science—as it is presently constituted— necessarily involves cruelty to animals. Every year, millions of frogs are dissected in high school classes in the name of learning biology. This annual ritual has undoubtedly contributed to the near-extinction of these unfortunate creatures, in addition to the general ecological decay and the export of frog's legs. School suppliers of frogs have a hard time finding them, but dissection continues to be treated as a sacrosanct and compulsory activity. In an encouraging incident in Bengal, suppliers of frogs to schools had to face stiff resistance from villagers.

It is ironical that school education should contribute to ecological decay rather than arouse critical awareness towards it. Studying the impact of violence on animals and plants could just as well form a part of the objective study of nature. Observation of animal behaviour is a highly advanced branch of modern science which hardly finds any room in our school programmes. Indeed, there is something deeply anti-nature in the prevailing concept of science education. Our system is committed to an old, mechanistic conception of science which sits well with entrenched pedagogic practices such as rote learning and testing of factual knowledge. The uses of science to nurture a sense of wonder and as an opportunity to enhance human ingenuity for tracing new links in familiar phenomena are alien to our system. It is hardly surprising that we are overawed by the progress of science and technology in the wealthier nations of the West. Learning of science ought to impart self-confidence, but in our case, it imparts nervousness and a sense of backwardness in comparison to the Western world. The lack of sensitivity towards the environment that we see in our science curricula is only a symptom of this deeper problem.

6

Let Us All Blame the Teacher

Blaming the teacher is so convenient, I wonder why people who are adept at the blame game bother to find other reasons for the state education is in. Aren't teachers insincere, lazy, incompetent, and indifferent to every criticism? Even as I begin to write this piece, I am acutely aware of the inevitable absence of teachers and teacher educators among my implied readers. Maybe a handful (literally) of teachers serving in highly select public schools might find access to this piece of writing in *The Book Review*, but there is hardly any chance that a rural teacher would be among my readers. The likelihood of an urban teacher serving in a government school or even a Kendriya Vidyalaya is also quite low. Let us face the fact that schoolteachers are not considered an intellectual workforce in our country. We don't expect schoolteachers to engage with matters of policy and theory. The image of a children's teacher we carry is of someone who keeps children under control and teaches the prescribed textbook. I am not surprised that the Chattopadhyaya Commission report has been virtually erased from policy memory, unlike the Kothari Commission which wrote its report two decades before the former but continues to be remembered and referred to. One reason why the report of the National Commission on Teachers, chaired by Professor D.P. Chattopadhyaya, has been forgotten could well be that its stress

on treating school teaching as a professional responsibility finds
no resonance in our social and policy ethos. 'Anyone can teach
children' is a commonly held opinion as well as policy reflected
in the status of teachers and in the conditions under which
they do their daily work. There is no point wasting space on
the crippling circumstances in which rural teachers fulfill their
daily duties. Consider the relatively better off public school
teacher of an urban metropolis. The grind of daily life involves
teaching six to seven periods a day, six days a week. Where is
the time to read a book or *The Book Review*?

Let us now look at teacher educators, and why they too are
unlikely to be among my readers. Teacher training institutions
constitute a world quite far removed from the world of
reflective writing like this one, books which arouse thought
and films which move. Why that should be so, and what are
its implications for the teachers trained at these institutions
are the two questions I will attempt to answer in this article.
Let me first share a fact. For a meeting of the State Council of
Educational Research and Training (SCERT) directors, held a
few months ago, the NCERT acquired a copy of *Pather Panchali*.
The morning after its screening the fact surfaced that except
for the West Bengal director, no one had seen it earlier, indeed
very few were aware of its existence or significance. It did
achieve what Ray had wanted it to, more than half a century
ago; that is, it gave people new eyes to perceive children
with, and a somewhat new frame of mind to look at village
childhood. However, no one could have any reason to feel
reassured that *Pather Panchali*'s magic could filter down, below
the level of directors, to swamp the staff of SCERTs, District
Institutes of Education and Training (DIETs), block and cluster
resource centres, and that other, parallel world of directorates
of education. And there is no point in making the last sentence
any longer by mentioning private teacher training institutions
which are mushrooming by the day, taking full advantage of the
onslaught of commercialization and corruption in this invisible
sector of education.

At the bottom of these two absences lies the assumption that teaching is a technique. A whole century has gone by without the instrumentalist character of teacher training (they now call it teacher education, in the hope that renaming will make a difference) being challenged or reformed. The late nineteenth-century ethos in which mechanistic theories of education held centre stage shaped the early teacher training practices. The normal schools, as they were called, emphasized lesson planning and delivery as the heart of teaching. By the time child psychology and progressive perspectives in the philosophy of education emerged as significant developments in the European world, the institutional codes in our colonial setting had already hardened. They got further reinforced with the advent of behaviourism as an overarching shell. It proved impervious to the cognitive revolution of the post-war decades. And quite recently, in the early twenty-first century, when the National Curriculum Framework briefly portrayed the child as a constructor of knowledge, even the politically progressive lot screamed at this blasphemy. Sustaining the scream was lack of faith in teachers, especially in their capacity to think and take decisions. The idea that teachers should be asked to integrate children's immediate world and their own thoughts and theories into classroom discourses struck many as an invitation to anarchy and relicensing of long outlawed practices like sati. If the arcane debate showed one thing with clarity, it was that the progressive and productive intellectual who might be a regular reader and writer of magazines like *The Book Review* does not trust the vast population of teachers and teacher trainers. Forget about decentralization and all other politically correct discourses of governance; when it comes to children's education, a command system appears best suited for the Republic of India in the fifty-eighth year of her independence from colonial rule. You can imagine the perils of being futuristic in an ethos in which political progressivism serves as so perfect and legitimate a mask for pedagogic conservatism.

Let us not be surprised if we find that people who habitually read novels, short stories, poetry, or feel anxious to keep in touch with research on children and education form a microscopic minority among those who teach teachers how to teach. Institutions of teacher training are not expected to have a functional library. Indeed, if you are talking about DIETs, which constitute a prime link in the chain of policy implementation, the physical condition of their buildings will make you seriously embarrassed as a citizen. And if you look at the newly licensed private outfits doling out B.Ed. degrees, you may not find a building in many cases. But even in the best teacher training institutions, some of which belong to universities, the idea that reading must form a routine practice does not hold. It is nobody's concern how ideas will circulate or percolate in the absence of reading. Books that discuss new practices adopted by adventurous NGOs do not reach these institutions. Indeed, there is no regard for NGO activity in the B.Ed./M.Ed. world. Both these degree programmes are structured around the faith that there is a certain way of doing things, that there is no need to apply one's mind when you have learnt that approved way. A craft-like perfection is attempted during the training, and once the training is over, it is assumed that the ideals of the craft cannot be applied in the setting of a real school. The rare B.Ed. degree-holder who walks out of her training institute into the real world of a school classroom, with the desire to apply her skills, soon discovers that no one else in the school believes this to be an attempt with any worth. Covering the syllabus, preparing children for examination, keeping them busy with homework, treating the annual function as the sole reason to worry about creative talent become the norm, and the planned lessons of B.Ed. days become a memory.

The second question, about the implications of a mechanistic model of teacher training, is now easy to answer. The basic implication is that training makes no difference. It remains a nominal achievement, a diploma or degree which makes you eligible for a job, but carrying no substantial value. The skills learnt are rooted in a concept of teaching that has little relevance to the children of today or to the policy framework guiding education. On values and attitudes, the training process makes no impact; indeed, it is not intended to. The values imbibed from the dominant worldview of society are never challenged, so the young, trained teacher does not relate to policies which require a radical shift in values and attitudes. For instance, inclusive schooling requires a totally fresh perception of intelligence and ability. The dominant Darwinian view that only a few have talent is contradictory to the policy framework, yet it prevails because schools are rooted in it.

Educational recovery crucially depends on the restoration of our faith in teachers. If we merely blame them for being incompetent and lazy, we won't get very far. In a recent conversation I heard an eminent, senior historian say that most of our teachers are communal. I am sure we can heap various other abuses on the teacher, determined as we are to ignore the real world of the school classroom where living children arrive from homes which are part of the contemporary world. Quite a few do not eat anything before coming to attend classes. Some do not get adequate sleep. Some face daily violence, and almost all are exposed to the relentless demonstration of violence on television. The teacher alternates her role all day to negotiate the world through her children, serving as healer, nurse, parent, police, and so on. Those who criticize the teacher should try spending a full day with fifty children. The number is usually higher; in many parts of India, it exceeds eighty. If teachers don't go mad, it is because they don't attempt the impossible. They manage as best as they can, keeping India's human resource development a low-energy operation. We can hardly hope to change this situation unless we look at teaching from the teacher's viewpoint, standing with her in a real, average school.

7

Two Memoirs of a Sporting Event

June, 2010

The law endowing on India's children a right to education (RTE) carried a date. So did the decision to host the Commonwealth Games in Delhi. For the vast number of out-of-school children of this city, the law has brought no change. When the schools re-open next week after the summer break, they will be no better prepared to receive and retain the thousands of children who have either never enrolled or who were eliminated by the system. Nor will life at school be any more child-friendly for those who have got used to the cramped, often cruel, conditions of Delhi's municipal schools. The authorities have made no preparation for implementing the new law which seeks to transform India's schools and end the apartheid that divides private from state-run schools. Under RTE, all private schools, and even Kendriya Vidyalayas, were supposed to offer one-fourth of their presently available seats to children of the poor living in the vicinity. Some private schools of Delhi have done this following an earlier court order, and some have made a provision for an afternoon shift for the poor which violates RTE. Kendriya Vidyalayas have taken no steps whatsoever, and the Pratibha Vikas Vidyalayas, for which the

Delhi Government screens children at Class VI, are carrying on with this practice. This too violates RTE.

It can be justifiably argued that the scale of systemic changes RTE demands would require a gestation period of more than the three months that have elapsed since the promulgation of RTE. Fair enough, but one cannot miss the contrast in the preparations made for RTE and those for the Commonwealth Games. The authorities have put in an extraordinary effort to stage these games in October. Quite literally, no stone in Delhi has been left unturned to make the event a historic achievement of national glory. The contrast between apathy to RTE and anxiety for the Games reveals the official meaning of national pride. True, the Commonwealth Games are a one-time event whereas RTE involves a vast, sustained effort. Both called for a massive investment in physical infrastructure. Preparation for implementing RTE would mean judicious deployment of available resources and mobilization of new ones. Neither process has begun. In the case of the Commonwealth Games, officials have gone overboard to squander a pumped up emergency budget to dress up Delhi in time to stage the Games.

Not just the venues where the Games will be held and people will stay, but the city at large is undergoing expensive plastic surgery. Roads and sidewalks are being dug up and redone. Wherever you look, piles of freshly purchased tiles waiting to replace the existing ones greet you. Parsimony is out; extravagance is in. All along Willingdon Crescent (now known after Mother Teresa), raised flowerbeds are being installed. For this, the beautiful and extensive sweep of well-maintained grass stretching from Teen Murti House to Lohia Hospital is being removed. Terraced flowerbeds and tiles will cover the stretch. Tiles seem to be the favourite among contractors and officials. Even the ones installed only last year are being replaced. The surroundings of India Gate are witnessing a similar relaying of perfectly acceptable sidewalks with garish cement tiles and sandstone curbs. The story of the Delhi University campus is probably the saddest. Here, an angular, tall rugby stadium now

stands facing the old Vice-regal Lodge which had been restored
to its original architectural ambience only three years ago at an
enormous expense. Hundreds of mature trees were cut down
to build an ugly parking lot. Access to it has been provided
by destroying another park which, till now, had marked the
university's platinum jubilee.

No doubt the chaos will soon settle down. Glitter of the
Games will erase the memory of all doubts and dilemmas.
The city will go on, coping with its endemic problems like
chronic water shortage, air pollution and lack of sanitation.
Both the manner and the style in which preparation for the
Commonwealth Games has proceeded will exacerbate Delhi's
problems. Let us take water shortage, for instance. All along
the freshly tiled sidewalks a strip has been left open for flower
bushes. Who will water them after the Games? The dried up
beds will remind children going to school that sustainable
development is a nice slogan and a topic to elaborate for
marks. The bricked tree enclosures erected to welcome
Queen Elizabeth a few years ago along her route soon became
convenient garbage dumps. During the days ahead of US
President Clinton's visit, a magistrate was sent around in a van
to fine anyone throwing garbage on the street. Each time such
a thing is done, we bring back to life the British stereotype of
Indians as people who will starve and save for years in order
to spend millions on a wedding night. It seems as if we have
learnt no lesson whatsoever about the meaning of modernity
as an exercise of reason and judgement for human goals. Had
these been applied for the staging of Commonwealth Games,
the staging could have been planned differently, with austerity
and warmth, to convey India's original vision and priorities
as a nation committed to equality among people and a new
world order.

Schools are going to stay closed during the Games. Afterwards
when they open again, sports will remain as inaccessible and
exotic as they are now for the majority of children. Playtime
will be cut in general, to make up for the closure during the

Games. In schools which have the misfortune to be located in the vicinity of a stadium or practice grounds, life has been tough. In one such government school, the sports ground was used for storing cement, bricks and sand for developing a nearby Commonwealth practice field. The Games' contractor chopped down the volleyball poles and left the ground littered with rubbish. For a whole session, children could not play. The coming session promises no relief. This school was lucky to have a playground. Most schools in Delhi have none. And college students are only slightly better placed in this respect. Inspiring the young was apparently not intended to be an outcome of the Games. Like everyone else, children were expected to act as spectators of a five-star extravaganza.

RTE represents the Republic's dream of recognizing every child as an active learner and a national asset. The law assiduously lists the systemic conditions that must be met to let this dream be realized. These conditions include a room for every class, special classes for older children who were never enrolled, one : thirty teacher-pupil ratio, higher qualifications and in-service training for every teacher, and a child-friendly environment in the school. A lot of hard work should—and could—have been done to meet RTE standards in Delhi's schools *before* April 1 when the law was to come into force. Now, after the summer break too, schools and teachers will be no better prepared to receive the tens of thousands of additional children that the RTE intends to bring into the system. Nor will teachers have any clearer understanding of what it means to allow children from diverse socio-economic backgrounds to study together. Private schools will continue grooming children of the richer classes for elite roles. Not one school in Delhi has emulated the example of Sister Cyril's historic achievement of turning the Loreto school in Calcutta into an exemplar institution where children of the poor study with the rich. Many corporate houses have now entered into the business of running schools. Fitted with centralized air-conditioning and close-circuit television cameras, these schools are chilling symbols of India's new apartheid culture. Under this culture, the poor have been thrown out to the margins of cities like Delhi. Their children are supposed to be content with the sub-human conditions which prevail in schools meant only for the poor. RTE rejects this situation and seeks to transform it so that education becomes a means of accelerating social cohesion rather than conflict. Governments of Bihar, Uttar Pradesh and Madhya Pradesh, among others, have declared that they do not have the funds to meet RTE norms. Delhi Government might do the same. Never mind the tiles.

November, 2010

Now that the terms of inquiry into the conduct of the Commonwealth Games have been extended, let us hope that the process of probe will be more open than was decision-making for the CWG. Let us also hope that the review will cover the opening and closing ceremonies as well, both in terms of their content and the decisions and choices involved in the actual design of these major cultural events. Both ceremonies received wide acclaim but left many citizens like me a bit terrified and confused. There were uplifting moments, but there was something deeply upsetting too. I felt as if the core of my identity as an Indian was going through an unexpected surgery. I could not stop feeling that an India I knew was being declared dead. Who had taken the decision to do so, I wonder. The Games are over and the propaganda of national prestige cannot be used anymore to silence dissenting voices. Let us revisit the experience of witnessing the dramatic changes this historic event introduced in the ethos of our country and its capital.

It was early in the morning and the year was 2008. During my daily walk, I noticed that someone had dug a trench around the tree I used to pass each day. Many roots were exposed. I thought perhaps the botany department of my university had decided to cure this tree of some root infection. The next day

I saw similar trenches around more trees, and within that week I noticed that the root systems had been bundled up in white plastic. Evidently, the trees were about to be relocated. One by one, over the next few weeks, hundreds of beautiful mature trees thus treated disappeared, leaving open holes in the ground. Pre-dawn trucks carried them away to an unknown destination. It was a kind of emergency. No one knew what was happening and how many trees would eventually go. It was rumoured that the contractor shifting these trees earned Rs.10,000 per tree. There was no way of verifying this or anything else that happened over the next three years on the campus of Delhi University and in other parts of the city. Let the inquiry committee find out how many trees survived the shifting and where they now are. I would certainly like to visit them if they are alive. Even if they are found dead, which is likely, it would be a relief to have the mystery surrounding their relocation unravelled.

How Delhi's public learnt to endure the pervasive but unexplained disruption of their daily life and the wilful destruction of the environment cannot be easily assessed or documented. A sudden loss of common civic rights took place. It was sometimes described as a kind of 'sacrifice,' but the idea of sacrifice includes acceptance of a cause and attribution of greatness to it. Not for a day did the cause look great. When the display part of the ordeal was over, some people expressed pride and pleasure. For them as well as for all the others, it is important to remember that the consequences of the ordeal will stay for years and debates will be necessary to determine what exactly the Games meant for the nation. This is why it is important to recall what preceded the event and happened during it. I remember the day the Platinum Jubilee park on the campus was closed and decimated so that it could be converted into a parking lot. There was no discussion, no mention of the cost it had incurred only a few years ago. It was clear that the people who had taken over were far more powerful than the ordinary residents of the area and students. When the

2010 session began, the students were blocked from their own hostels. Several buildings were demolished. Telephone cables were repeatedly slashed, electricity and water supply was disrupted, and traffic turned into chaos. On the sidewalks, the Games took the form of a festival for contractors dealing in tiles. New tiles were installed in millions and in every conceivable colour and design. Old tiles, even the ones laid out a few months ago, were dug out. Towards the end, the tile-diggers went berserk and replaced the ones they had placed a few weeks ago. Rickshawpullers and street vendors were treated like pests—to be hit any hour of the day when the authorities wanted the road to look world class. Construction workers were made to work day and night; many who got sick, injured or died were made to disappear.

Civic and social costs apart, the financial cost of the Games will remain difficult to judge. Towards the final months, the media gave a glimpse of the scale of corruption involved in the procurement of utilities, but even if we leave those stories aside, the legitimate expenditure raises fundamental questions about the nation's priorities and values. Estimates vary but the average figure is astounding. It exceeds the total annual contribution of the Centre to the Sarva Shiksha Abhiyan (SSA). How will the government convince anyone that India's ability to turn its children's right to education into a reality is hampered by a budget constraint? Why would the tribal people of Jharkhand and Chhattisgarh, who are fighting with their backs against the wall, believe that their country lacks the resources to rehabilitate them with dignity when mining companies require them to be thrown off their forest land? The profligacy exhibited in the Games signifies the state's seal of approval of the lifestyle of India's new maharajas. There is no point now fantasizing that we can persuade Mukesh Ambani to gift his 27-storey house and its hanging gardens to Mumbai's children as a vertical amusement park. What he has spent out of his own earnings is merely half the SSA's annual central outlay.

The callous financial behaviour was matched by the gross

choices made in the representation of culture. A key item of the closing ceremony was the electronic representation of a giant size woman dancing in the nude. The item was reputedly imported from Germany, along with a team of laser technicians. It was truly a crowning moment—in the history of a society being engineered by determined hands. Exactly whose hands they are is hard to say, and that is why this is a memoir of feeling disoriented and shaken. Perhaps the inquiry committee will find out who approved that laser show and the Bollywood dance which followed. Let it also ascertain the justification for the decision to ask the young women who carried the medals for distribution to victorious athletes to dress themselves in a bridal *lehenga*. If the inquiry process throws even modest light on such choices, it will help to make sense of the leap we have taken in the dark, deluded in the name of the nation and its glory.

In the opening ceremony, there were items displaying the Buddha and Gandhiji. We do need to construct, with memory and imagination, what *they* would have thought of the indignity meted out to womanhood in the laser show of the closing ceremony. Those who choreographed the closing ceremony do not distinguish between women's bodies and common utilities. They apparently attribute sovereignty to the male right to consume both as the basic point of India's current economic growth. As philosopher and historian Lata Mani has pointed out, we are witnessing the rise of a new kind of body politic which is hostile to the Constitution's vision of a nation which guarantees dignity to all —*including* women and children, not just men. If the state is the primary instrument of realizing that vision, the Games have certainly damaged the state's credibility. It will take a long and patient effort to restore public confidence in the state's decisions to the pre-Games level. It was not particularly high, cynics might say, but even they would agree that the Games have injured civic faith. Whatever can be done to heal that injury should be done.

The World Around

8

Future Girls

The idea of a residential school for girls evokes the image of prim uniforms and stern discipline. The Kasturba School I saw in Saharanpur last month flouts the image, at least for now. It is one of the ten schools Mahila Samakhya is running in different parts of Uttar Pradesh (UP) for village girls who 'dropped out' of school early. Mahila Samakhya started in 1992 in twenty-one blocks spread over different regions of UP. I had read about its reputation for reshaping rural women's identity but nothing had prepared me for what I saw in Saharanpur.

As of now, the Kasturba School does not have its own building, so it runs in a rented house with three large rooms, one small room which serves as office space and a guava tree. The tiny veranda outside has four easy chairs of the kind made in Saharanpur—elegant and comfortable, communicating a sense of care and honesty one seldom sees in mainstream schools. For lunch I had the food served to the girls. I attended three classes, first mathematics, then science and language. The active engagement I saw in the mathematics class was stunning. One forgot that the students are from the poorest sections of rural society, that they are primary school dropouts, that the class was being taken in one of India's most challenging states in terms of literacy and schooling. This class could make an American or French teacher envious. The teacher stayed relaxed and confident while the girls measured each other's height, recording it in small groups for further analysis. In other classes too, the teacher knew exactly what her role was—to suggest the next step, supervise, and expedite the work being done in groups.

Later in the day I met some fifty coordinators of different activities in the ten districts where Mahila Samakhya exists. This is when I learnt about the living reality of the reports I had read, about the 'nari adalat' (women's court)[1] programme in which women investigate criminal cases to sharpen them for court proceedings. I had heard stories about the leadership given by rural women in harsh social circumstances. Women like Ramjani have fought for the rights of other women in a milieu where the networks that metropolitan activists assume are a fantasy. The extraordinary achievement of Mahila Samakhya in UP lies in its persistence and faith in eventual victory over social and administrative inertia. The only question that remains is whether its style of honest and rigorous functioning can influence the larger system of state education.

Schools in UP run like any other wing of the government. They are splendidly insulated from the deep churning one sees in social and economic relations. In many parts of rural UP, teachers face the challenge of managing impossibly large classes. Shortage of teachers and rational deployment of those available are chronic problems. Outside the system, one can find a number of experiments, including Mahila Samakhya, which show that systemic flexibility is essential if we want to accommodate children from the poorest classes of society. Several innovative attempts are currently on under Sarva Shiksha Abhiyan (SSA). In several other states too, alternative schooling models are being tried out for children in India. The

[1] A practice initiated under the Mahila Samakhya programme, in which an all-women's court makes an independent investigation into crimes against women.

lessons learnt differ, but one thing is applicable throughout the country, namely, that the mainstream school system learns nothing from these experiments. Its daily timetable, the annual cycle of teaching and examination as well as the methods of teaching and record-keeping have resisted any influence of the numerous innovative experiences of alternative models.

Softening of this resistant character of the school system forms the core of the NCF, 2005. It flags flexibility in all aspects of school life and policy. Flexibility means responsiveness to local requirements and changes. It also means strategies like subsidiarity and participation in decision-making. Basically, the NCF is a plea for bringing the school system into the fold of larger administrative and financial reforms, giving greater autonomy to the teacher in a new frame of stronger linkages between parental bodies and the school. Changes of this nature require a great deal of popular support for the cause of children's education, which is not easy to muster. The kind of community mobilization Mahila Samakhya has achieved is unthinkable at present in the context of government schools. Their listless life and the common stories of corruption in the utilization of funds make the community cynical. But there is no alternative.

The old inspector raj can hardly be expected to shed its corruption and lethargy. The plea for further erosion of the state system, because it is not accountable is equally false. Reform of the state schools by focusing on generous inputs into infrastructure and pedagogy, on one hand, and conscientization of the parental community, on the other, are worthy courses of action. In this line, the Mahila Samakhya experience offers substantial hope. Let us place all government schools under the supervisory authority of Mahila Samakhya in the districts where it is active in UP. Its heroic record of instilling pride and self-confidence in rural women leaders must be put to wider use.

In a couple of years we will begin to see the results. Of course, the move will be resisted, for the interests vested in the status quo are quite substantial. Nor should we underestimate the power of inertia which inevitably takes the form of negative energy when things are nudged. The idea that awakened, activist women will assume authority over government schools will arouse male ire within the system as well as outside it. But UP has already come a long way with Mahila Samakhya and can venture a step further.

Apart from multiplying schools of this kind, we need to imagine an alternative future for the girls of Saharanpur's Kasturba School. After they finish what is equivalent to grade eight at the Kasturba School, requiring them to go back to the so-called mainstream of education, would be sad indeed. Even if UP decides one day to reform its school education along the lines suggested in the NCF, tangible results would take a long time to surface. Meanwhile, the Kasturba School girls will have to endure the rigid curriculum and uninspiring pedagogy of ordinary schools. Let us imagine that some of them survive this test of endurance. What next, other than matrimony? Those few who might have the stamina to enrol for college education will end up in the traditional BA course which has little to offer to a rural girl except the pleasure of possessing a degree.

I would like to imagine an adventurous alternative—the beginning of a rural women's university where the Kasturba School girls and others like them might strive for a truly higher education of a different sort. The present system of higher education has no place for village girls. An estimate made a few years ago had calculated that just about one, out of every hundred rural girls who enrol in the first grade, survives in the system long enough to take the twelfth grade examination. This situation has not changed much, partly because rural schools are in poor shape in most parts of India barring exceptions like Kerala, Karnataka, and Himachal Pradesh, but mainly because the curriculum has so little to offer to rural children, especially girls. There are a few rural universities in the country, but none of them represents an extension of an innovative school-age education programme. The Kasturba schools run under the Mahila Samakhya programme present a precious opportunity to design a new kind of higher education for rural women whose pre-university education has occurred outside our stifling schools.

9

Democracy Without Democrats?

There never was much room for free—that is, fearless—speech and moral choices in the district towns. Between the collector and the police superintendent, the two prime symbols of the law-and-order state, the power to monitor life in the basti stayed finely tuned to the perspective of the local notables. That fine-tuning has loosened a little as a result of the local notables getting somewhat diversified. The loosening, however, has brought no relief to the limited tribe of the so-called local intelligentsia who yearn to exercise their right to free speech and association.

An unprecedented increase in the number of guns of every variety over the last two decades or so has made the district towns altogether unsuitable for the practice of enlightened enquiry into matters relevant to public welfare. Both administrative and political life in the district, at least in northern India, are steeped in corruption and civic disorder patronized by the powerful. None of the instruments of civil society have the strength to subject either power or authority to any kind of public scrutiny.

It sounds melodramatic and totally unacademic to say this, but the truth is that someone who lives in a district headquarter and does not appreciate the stringent limits within which the constitutional guarantees of free speech may be enjoyed, pays by getting roughed up or killed. Why many more are not killed is because life in a district town quickly socializes you to apply good sense. The stringent limits within which fearless speech can be practised are the four walls of your home.

Modern communication should have changed this picture for the better, and it has, so far as the exercise of brute force during elections is concerned. The possibility of sending a message to the chief election commissioner by phone or fax has curbed the earlier enthusiasm with which polling booths were captured. However, when the elections are over, the technology of speedy communication ceases to matter, for no one knows who in Bhopal or Delhi would bother.

The only institution which routinely uses communications technology is the local press, but it is hardly an institution in any serious sense. The local man who acts as correspondent to a regional or national daily is chronically under pressure to abandon every controversial matter after touching it once. In any case, there is no news in civic disorder, for it is a daily cycle. From a girl getting kidnapped to selection of teachers on bribe, no information is weightier than the subsidized newsprint that carries it to the saturated reader who does not even hope, anymore, that the collector or the chief minister will read it and bother to do anything. As for the locally published newspapers—there are literally thousands of them—they are much too dependent on the mercy of the local notables to enjoy or provide what we may call a liberal space.

District India has to stage a massacre, an epidemic, or a successful blockade of inter-regional transport to figure in the liberal space that our country has been lucky to have at the national level. Several historical struggles and breakthroughs are responsible for the creation and maintenance of this space, and we have every reason to be proud of it, especially if we look around for parallels. It is not just Pakistan and Iran that one thinks of as being less lucky than us, but the richer countries of South-east Asia too, which subsist on narrowly defined civic freedoms even as they boast of more open economies.

I feel similarly sorry for those who compare China with India and pronounce China has done better. I suppose civic freedom is a possession one appreciates only when one begins to see the danger of losing it. This is why I secretly feel happy when I hear people saying with anxiety that the liberal space is shrinking. I almost feel like saying, 'I'm glad it is, for now you can notice what we had.' I also feel like saying, 'Are you surprised?' Of course I say no such thing and be mistaken for a cynic.

As a true metropolitan, unlike a migrant from the hinterland which I am, you are supposed to say, 'Isn't that terrible.' The usual point of reference is one or the other news, such as the attack on that remarkably dull film, *Fire*, or the digging up of the Kotla cricket pitch. 'How objectionable!' you are supposed to exclaim, and get on with more substantial issues like why Murli Manohar Joshi does not want to win the hearts of college teachers or how *The Hindu* is now the only Delhi paper you can read.

It is indeed alarming how trivial an issue we make of the rapid erosion of the freedom of intellectual and moral choices, speech and association. Why the erosion does not surprise me is on account of four trends that I have been aware of for some time now. The first of these is the only one to have surfaced in the recent past, especially since the display of unreluctant patronage of globalization policies by the Rao–Singh regime. The other three trends have been around for much longer, though two of them were not as perceptible earlier as they are now. The fourth one is still quite invisible because it stays hidden in every child's schoolbag, which is quite a treasure of national security secrets in our country.

But let me start with the first reason which I wish to call the commoditization of the media. It is distinct from commercialization which is a part of life, monetized life at any rate. Commoditization, on the other hand, is new and sinister, an aspect of neo-colonialism inasmuch as it denies us the right to choose and apply our minds.

The slogan of globalization symbolizes a new incarnation of the European psyche, this time under American command. The incarnation has two faces. One is the intellectually and ethically tired face, showing that the white man now wishes to drop his burden, more out of a desire to enjoy his own life fully with his two boxes, TV and PC, than out of any moral realization of odium in the burden or a recognition of the futility of carrying it. The other is the face with sophisticated aggression, conveying the right of property over all sorts of resources that can be bought and ideas that can be sold for money. This second face is cruder than the plunderers of the age of mercantile colonialism, or so it appears to us, who had not imagined that the West, with its great universities and museums, could come to this, again.

The degree of consensus there is about globalization having become man's destiny now, from company managers to human rights groups in the West, is quite amazing, though it is in keeping with the European world's compulsion to invent something to get euphoric about every couple of decades. What this consensus means for us is a denial of choice in everything, including globalization itself. We are being told that this time there is no getting away with selective absorption, that everything comes with everything else, that we must sit back and be happy that we can at least manipulate the mouse in our right hand.

Commoditization of the media is a component of this latest round of the West's chronic obsession with new toys and slogans on one hand, and of a distinct move by a handful of corporate interests towards consolidation of their dominance on the other. Our media managers and state media bureaucrats cannot contain their excitement. They now see their primary role in acting like conduits for advertising. As CNN does day and night, most of our newspapers and glossies are using bits of news to sell advertising. They are using precious newsprint to promote every object there is in the dung heap—from cigarettes to junk food, from music systems our walls have no substance to contain inside buildings to cars our cities have no space to park or drive with safety. Both news and views are treated as commodities in these publications; therefore, a debate on public health or destruction of the environment must compete for space with Coca-Cola and car advertisements. A large section of the press now regards sustained debate on issues of public importance as being marginal to its main business which is to push the induction of Indian elites into global consumerism.

One might have seen this as a matter of choice on the part of our media owners and bureaucrats had it not been obvious that global media and communication barons have been specifically after us. On the other hand, I wish I could say that our people have been forced into submission, to reprint or adapt junk writing from the American or British press and trivia from the fashion industry. Unfortunately, neither version of what happened is adequate. An ethos existed which made commoditization of the media acceptable. That ethos made elaborate debates or enquiry look boring. Once that ethos started to grow, few seemed to have the strength to resist it.

Post-Rajiv Gandhi political happenings played their role (some might say, post-Indira Gandhi); economic forces supportive of the change had been active since the mid-1970s. By the beginning of the current decade, political consensus had been established that colonialist modernism was the only choice left for us to follow. I believe this consensus had its basis in the loss of popular mandate suffered by all national-level parties, but that is a different issue. For the construction of the ethos which made commoditization of the media acceptable, we must turn to the next two reasons which, in addition to their ethos-building role, were directly responsible as well for the shrinking of the liberal space.

When Salman Rushdie wrote, in *The New Yorker*'s special issue on free India's golden jubilee, that he reads no Indian language well enough to read its literature, but, never mind, he knew that nothing worthwhile had been written in any of these languages in recent times, he was saying something I could have associated with some of my colleagues and friends whose reading for news and pleasure is confined to English. It is just nice that they lack Rushdie's arrogance.

Growing up in an Indian city without having any substantial exposure to the literature of the region to which the city belongs was a familiar feature of the public school student's personality, but the walls dividing the English-educated intelligentsia and its vernacular counterpart have got thicker and taller of late. The vernacular media have virtually no place in the institutions serving the English-educated intellectual elite who depend on English both for receiving news and for responding to it. They have no direct access to the articulation of the public mind which takes place in the vernacular media and literature. Of course there are famous exceptions, but they are exceptions.

The gap between English and the vernacular is perhaps wider in the Hindi heartland than elsewhere, but it exists in other parts of India in varying measures. It is related to the trend towards divisiveness we see in other contexts too, but it has special significance because of its function in shaping the flow of information. I recall the sudden despair into which a number of English-dependent social analysts were thrown by the events that preceded and followed the Ayodhya disaster. I generally find it a waste of time to look at an English newspaper to find out what is happening in Uttar Pradesh. On the other side of the language wall, I miss the generation of Rajendra Mathur, Raghuvir Sahay, Agyeya, and S.C. Dube, who wrote in Hindi with a vast and confident awareness of what was being written in English. Liberal press and scholarship in Hindi stand greatly impoverished by the absence of such people. On the other hand, the lack of direct and habitual access to the vernacular world limits both the knowledge and the sensibility that the commentators writing in English can put to use in their professionally and socially significant tasks.

The wall that divides the intelligentsia is symbolic of the divisions that have been growing in the larger urban middle class, irrespective of where it resides. Its upper layers, which include those with power and status as well as the upwardly mobile, have lost all but ritual links with the vernacular world to which they once belonged. This is evident from their orbits of awareness, interests, reading, child rearing, and objects of desire. The areas where they reside in cities have hardly any trace of the local literary milieu.

If you were to make a foolish query at Teksons in Delhi's South Extension market for Krishna Sobti's *Dilo Daanish*, you would be looked at with contempt and not just surprise, unless you were a foreigner who did not know that bookshops in Delhi are not like the ones in Rome which mostly stock books in Italian. Down at the district level, you can guess who gets the few copies of the English original of *India Today*. The collector and some of his colleagues are sometimes the only ones who keep in touch with the English media.

If they also keep an eye on the local and regional vernacular press, it is mainly to equip themselves with the knowledge of ground reality which they are literally supposed to control as custodians of law and order. For status maintenance and mental nourishment they depend on the English media which inevitably provides them the lexicon of current civil dialogue. This lexicon is rather distant from the world of their 'grass-roots' subordinates, such as members of the panchayat, primary schoolteachers, health workers, and unemployed youth acting as volunteers in a state programme. These subordinates inhabit a purely vernacular world which generates, off the numerous cutting edges of development, a lexicon of its own. The collector and his colleagues inevitably have a hollow ring in their utterances when they address these armies of development. Many civil servants are nowadays writing about their 'grass-roots' experiences in journals like the *EPW*, and there too the hollow ring dogs their words. They lack the language capable of sizing up the corruption, the fear, and the silent violence that surround the sundry initiatives taken by the state to get closer to the people. The interface between the authorities and the state's own modest instruments of serving the people messes up the little liberal space there is in district headquarters. And we are not even talking about the guns and the goons monitoring the financial flows for welfare.

Let me turn to the third and the fourth reasons, both of which have to do with the general erosion of educational values. Especially relevant to my present theme is the decline of higher education and the use of school education for ideological propaganda. Active political misuse of provincial universities is now an old story. But it gives us a framework that is still relevant for looking at the systemic neglect of post-secondary education. Apart from motivated misuse by politicians, higher education has also suffered the spread of poor quality primary and secondary education.

The thin layer of free and somewhat informed dialogue that the college teacher and students had sustained in places which had no bookshops, vanished during the Emergency of the mid-1970s; it never materialized again. Radical budget cuts of the 1980s made a vital contribution to the dismantling of the college ethos, particularly by affecting library supplies. Today, a working library is a preserve of privileged universities; others must do with the oral tradition and bazaar notes. During a recent visit I realized with dismay that an old, highly respected institution like Allahabad's Ewing Christian College was not even expected to have a decent library.

India's higher education establishment, oversized though it was in relation to the sea of illiteracy surrounding it, had produced since its inception in colonial days a great body of men and women who acted as conflict managers in a diversified and segmented society. As lawyers, civil servants, teachers, journalists, and members of voluntary groupings, they oiled the wheels and gears of our difficult democracy during its formative phases with their skills of civil disagreement and representation of positions. Financially depleted and poorly governed, higher education still produces any number of qualified young adults, but these skills have become rarer. And now, under the World Bank's persuasion, an argument has gained ground that India needs literacy and elementary education more urgently than it needs serious higher education.

Pernicious as it is, this argument ignores the social history of our democracy. Of course our universities have a lot to answer for in the stagnated frames of knowledge they continue to maintain. Nor can we say that as institutions they have rendered meaningful service to the recent processes of social change. But their presence in a society with so much fighting has been a stabilizing and nurturing influence. One can say that democracy does not depend on them, for the norms and procedures of democracy have struck deeper roots. However, democracy without democrats to defend it will always remain fragile. It may not die, but it will waste a lot of energy in survival alone. It may not die also because democracy has proved the most convenient form of governance for India, but its survival as a form of governance is not enough to make it a way of life.

Finally, let us look at the use of school education for promoting mindless acceptance of the stated. Who is behind it, I wonder, but it is happening all the time. Most probably no one in particular is behind it; our schools are merely transmitting what is supposed to be a dominant ideology. It is the same ideology that Aakaashvani and Doordarshan transmit in a more concrete sense.

Some important features of this ideology can help us recognize it, and they are as follows. The government knows best. It is following the best possible choices, especially in the context of India's development and security. Development generally means making India look like a copy of the West. If some part of a city begins to look faintly like a Western city, it can be seen and used as a symbol of development. Similarly, if agriculture gets firmly plugged into industries that produce chemical fertilizers, pesticides, and harvesters, this too is a sign of development. Poverty, the ideology says, is related to the outlook of the poor, their lifestyle, commitment to traditions, and superstitions. Generally, the poor, rural folk are to blame for their own condition.

This brief sketch should suffice to indicate the contours of the propaganda that schools are mounting all the time. It is not so much in the success or failure in this job that the problem lies; rather, it lies in their ignoring the other job, that of enabling children to make sense of the India that is unfolding. In that systematically ignored India, it is the rural masses who determine the outcome of elections; they resist and campaign against the unfair policies and one-sided initiatives of the state, thereby acting as correctives to state policy; they force development and modernization to take a specifically Indian shape. Our schools fail to present to the young an India which is an exciting place to live and work. On the contrary, they put across an image of India where only statesmen, civil servants, and scientists who act like civil servants matter. I recall the biography of a Nobel laureate Indian scientist which emphasized, for the benefit of elementary-level children, the fact of his being so brilliant that a commissioner of income tax decided to choose him as a son-in-law.

We can read deeper meanings—class hegemony and sinister foreshadows—in the school curriculum and the textbooks produced by the NCERT and the state bureaus. What is more important for now is to notice that the system is not designed to make children think. The approved policy of packing the maximum number of facts in the minimum space also gives a valid excuse to textbook-manufacturing bodies to leave no clues or room that might allow a young reader to stop and wonder about something.

The implied reader of these textbooks is someone who finds the world too cumbersome a place to make sense of; so it is best to leave it to the state to manage. Can we call such a reader a 'good citizen'? Such readers will undoubtedly be loyal to the authorities, but they can hardly be trusted as guardians of our turbulent democracy. If the liberal space has shrunk on issue after issue, good citizens of this kind and the system which produced them must take some responsibility.

10

A Memory of Coming to Life

Under Gandhi's leadership, the struggle against colonial rule evolved into an interesting sketch of what one might reasonably call a national culture. Those born between the second and the fourth decade of the twentieth century—roughly between 1915 and 1935—appear to have had a good chance to get acculturated into this during their childhood and youth in many parts of India. By the early 1940s, it was already a little too late as the embryonic stirrings of what I am trying to commemorate as a national culture were facing formidable challenges, if they were not already a fading force. Apparently, the social forces harnessed by the national movement under the Congress leapt into a make-believe maturity under Gandhi's charismatic and nurturant authority. When that authority started to wane, these forces receded into their juvenile state.

Independent India, with the elderly and de-graced Gandhi assassinated by a valid representative of the reaction he had triggered, was left with a national state without a cultural life backing it. Rabindranath Tagore had warned Gandhi about this possibility with cold precision, but there was little Gandhi could have done without stopping to be himself. Given the cleavages between his upbringing and his agenda by the scale of his achievement, one is hardly surprised by the limits of what he achieved; rather, one is shocked. Subsequent to the diminution of his authority and, finally, his forced disappearance, the social forces he had unleashed exhibited the lack of intrinsic motivation and the skills to conserve what they had attained. The stirrings of a national culture Indian society had heard in its deeper mind started to sink. A barren sound of the state's drum, under Nehru's sincere command, continued to remind the people that they had had a singing class.

Before I proceed to portray the substance of the fleeting phenomenon I have identified, I would like to devote some space to explicating the two terms, 'culture' and 'national'. Not that there are not enough definitions around, but in the kind of conditions that prevail in India today there is no harm in recalling the commonplace. That culture and the nation are both always and everywhere in the making—and not just in the so-called developing societies—can no more be regarded as an everyday truth. Children are being told to feel proud of India because it had a glorious culture in ancient times. In this ethos, it may feel strange to be reminded of the ordinary fact that cultures thrive on tacit knowledge, and therefore, the need to indulge in explicit glorification betokens death. We live in the age of documentation, an activity that necessarily implies the fear of losing something. It also contradicts the principle of knowledge, about life and the world (including aspects beyond our examining reach and reachable only with the help of imagination), which marks a living culture. The bulk of it must be tacit, and accessible only by sharing both space and life. Turning this larger part of the knowledge that a culture inheres into a description runs the risk of sounding absurd. Essentialisation, often through a process of reification, threatens to distort the proportions of ordinary matters beyond recognition. When words become the primary instrument of talking about a culture, the universe of understandings held tacitly together in a web of relationships is turned into a rational struggle.

76 A PEDAGOGUE'S ROMANCE

This unfortunate transformation is at the heart of the difficulty underlying the relationship between culture and education. The difficulty is so great that even decent, great theorists of education like Dewey and Tagore face it gingerly; others generally avoid it. The basic trouble is that education in modern conditions is a highly literate exercise: it depends so much on words that it cannot safeguard against essentializing whatever it deals with. The only safeguard education can offer are uncertain resources like the teacher's personality and the ethos of the institution. These resources become inaccessible when the teachers' selection, training, and conditions of work cease to require more than bureaucratic handling; and when the idea of an ethos becomes so unfashionable that the Internet is presented as an alternative to libraries, and gardens are maintained for announcing status, not for giving children a chance to look after plants and insects.

Luckily, both Gandhi and Tagore were aware of the tenuous linkage between education and culture, though their writing on this subject is shrouded in contemporary discourses.[1] Their ideas, and even more their practices, are important for us because education is in modern societies a prime instrument of what is customarily referred to as nation building. If nations need a cultural sketch to live by, the instrumental value of education for pencilling such a sketch will stay limited so long as teaching and learning are literacy-centred. Indeed, the use of education for nation building turns out to be quite self-evidently dangerous when nation building is undertaken by hostile neighbours like India and Pakistan. In both, education has become a ready-to-use tool for the destruction of culture. How these rather well-built nations will survive without living cultures is anybody's guess. But let me return to making one

[1] In her *Gandhi: His Gift of the Fight* (Friends Rural Centre, Hoshangabad, 1987), Marjorie Sykes provides some comparative insights into Gandhi and Tagore's ideas. She had worked with both.

more point about culture which I have borrowed from Mahadevi Verma.

Mahadevi Verma makes a distinction between the *nirmit* and the *nirmanadhin* aspects of culture and favours attention to the latter. We can translate these two Hindi terms of hers as, respectively, the 'finished' or 'built-up' and that which is 'under construction'. The former aspect of a culture commands admiration but symbolizes the principle of decay, literally because something already completed can only decline, whereas the latter aspect symbolizes change and growth, suggesting hope. The distinction assumes remarkable complexity when we place it in the context of Mahadevi Verma's definition of culture as a self-renewing energy. Culture, she says, is the means by which life in society purges or refines itself and which preserves the qualities born in the course of the purging. This is as close as I could get to translating Mahadevi Verma's tight Hindi prose; but I can do better by putting my own metaphorical gloss over it. We can elucidate her definition by regarding culture as a soap which rinses away the impurities resulting from the daily struggle of living; miraculously, the soap is made from the used, dirty rinse water. In this peculiar chemistry of culture, the messier or richer the rinse water, the more effective the soap. On the firm cybernetic ground of this metaphor stands the argument that a culture must remain mostly 'under-construction', or else it will hasten its own death.

Now to apply this logic of Mahadevi Verma's to retracing the Indian project, we notice that it concerned a gigantic reinvention by means of the intermixture of cultural specificities and the reduction of inequities. The chances of a national culture taking a form—without hurting other forms or substituting them, or in any way claiming to become the national culture—depended on the scale and the subtlety with which the intermixing would occur and the willingness with which inequities would be reduced. Implicit in these processes was the opening of religious, linguistic, and ethnic borders, the hastening of measures like land redistribution and the inclusion of Dalits in the apparatuses of the state and civil society. Directly hurting some and making many chronically sullen were necessary parts of the game initiated by the national movement, well before Gandhi's arrival. He made it look real, that is all; and that is what made the deadly difference. Angry and nervous about the rise of the downtrodden, the upper caste Hindu communities politicized themselves into a kind of counter-consciousness which nurtured the dream of an alternative national culture. It fed the already active search for cover among the Muslim elite.

Once formed, the state of free India offered security for individual freedom and an isolated mechanism for social justice. Neither was smoothly reconcilable with caste and patriarchy, both of which had sanction in religion. A voluntary and vast war on socially inherited structures of allegiance was the core national culture that surfaced between the second and the fourth decades of the twentieth century, shaping the socialization of countless individuals. Nationalism clearly offered a far wider programme than independence, and Gandhi's idea of swaraj was of a moral responsibility to rule ourselves differently from how the British had ruled us. Many people who grew up during those decades, especially women, lived life in ways not recognized earlier; others dreamed.

Tagore's delineation of the 'heaven of freedom' sketches that dream in two strokes: 'where the mind is without fear and the head is held high'. Gandhi's contribution towards making both these components of Tagore's dream a reality is a historical fact that probably no critic of his will choose to deny. He made common men and women capable of taking the mighty British Empire in their stride. This he did by selecting such ordinary things as salt and clothes as a symbolic venue for fighting against colonialism. But apart from the symbols he chose, his style—both in writing and living—had the gift of what Calvino (with, of course, no reference to Gandhi) calls 'lightness' in his last book, *Six Memos for the Next Millennium*. In the first memo, Calvino explains lightness as 'a value rather than a defect' in the context of his own efforts to 'remove weight, sometimes from people, sometimes from heavenly bodies, sometimes... from the structure of stories and from language'.[2] Calvino's memos were prepared in 1984; in Gandhiana we find plenty of examples that Calvino would have approved. His photograph taken outside the Buckingham Palace or the one with his hand on Lady Mountbatten's shoulder as they enter the Viceregal Lodge (both pictures are given in Louis Fisher's book on Gandhi)[3] offer us vivid examples of his determination (it hardly matters whether it was conscious or not) to take weight off powerful people. His confidence in his own dignity made the British look a little silly, and starkly unfair. This is how his own body and conduct became like salt and khadi—easy-to-read haikus of India's pride. Today we can hardly grasp this language without making a special effort simply because we have come a long way. Our children are now said to be in the need of being told about the Vedas and what mathematics they might contain, not to mention the Hindu ability to kill large numbers of Muslims in street encounters as displayed in Gujarat, in order to feel self-confident and secure. Gandhi's way was subtler.

The same could be said of his writing, if additional proof was needed to make the point. That it is possible to break out is conveyed in *Hind Swaraj*, not so much by meaning or assertion as by a cacophony of disagreements. I can imagine Gandhi's personality to be a bit like this book: ridiculously bold, yet so modest and graceful as to distract people from the extreme nature of his disapproval of established truths. Ambivalence was a necessary part of his strategy, and so was frequent shifting of position. This last characteristic has made Gandhi a victim of all-round appropriation; currently, it is the Hindu Right's turn; never mind that they killed him. They and their sympathizers can plentifully quote him on cow slaughter, Sanskrit, the *vama*

---

[2] Italo Calvino, *Six Memos for the New Millennium*, Vintage, New York, 1988, p. 3.

[3] Louis Fischer, *The Life of Mahatma Gandhi*, Granada, London, [1951] 1982.

system, and so on. One thing they cannot afford to imitate is his lightness which permitted him to be so inventive, and the total lack of which makes them so stodgy. Gandhi put people together around the hallucination of a nation no one could define except by saying it was worth trying out. People who acquired an instant citizenship of the India run by Gandhi's stick included energetic young minds like Nehru and a few million others who must have felt a little dizzy, yet driven. That is precisely what Tagore was worried about. Popular upsurge was fine, he thought, but without a cultivated mind to hold it, a dangerous rebound could occur. These are his words from an article on the charkha cult written in 1925.[4]

Some strong and widespread intoxication of belief among a vast number of men can suddenly produce a convenient uniformity of purpose, immense and powerful. It seems for the moment a miracle of a wholesale conversion; and a catastrophic phenomenon of this nature stuns our rational mind, raising high some hope of easy realisation that is very much like a boom in the business market. The amazingly immediate success is no criterion of its reality—the very dimension of its triumph having a dangerous effect of producing a sudden and universal eclipse of our judgment. Human nature has its elasticity, and in the name of urgency, it can be forced towards a particular direction far beyond its normal and wholesome limits. But the rebound is sure to follow, and the consequent disillusionment will leave behind it a desert track of demoralisation. We have had our experience of this in the tremendous exultation lately produced by the imaginary easy prospect of Hindu-Muslim unity. And therefore I am afraid of a blind faith on a very large scale in the charkha in the country, which is so liable to succumb to the lure of short cuts when pointed out by a personality about whose moral earnestness they can have no doubt.[5]

[4] Sabyasachi Bhattacharya, *The Mahatma and the Poet*, National Book Trust, New Delhi, 1997, pp. 101–2.
[5] R.K. Prabhu and Ravindra Kelekar (eds), *Truth Called them Differently*, Navjivan, Ahmedabad, 1961.

These were thoughts appropriate for a pedagogue. Tagore's awareness that learning takes time, that there is no substitute for it, extended to the infrastructure of custom and hierarchy, poverty and drudgery that predated colonial rule and were consolidated by it. Tagore was an artist as well, and his pedagogic experiments were unique in the emphasis they placed on the training of sensibility. Tagore and Gandhi came from two rather different universes of early socialization, and they acted and responded to many situations in dissimilar ways, but they recognized and prioritized the same issues as India's problems. Gandhi's campaign mode apparently filled Tagore with both awe and suspicion—awe for its splendid success, and suspicion in its residues. Tagore was afraid that Indian society would not change all that much under Gandhi's magic; it would only acquire a memory of coming to life.

The job of managing memory is normally done in modern conditions by the system of education. It is a difficult job, but who needs to be reminded of that in the year 2002 when the highest court in the land failed to protect India's children from resolute and unscrupulous manipulators of memory? To preserve the rich and complex memory of the national culture brought alive in the Gandhi era of the freedom struggle was a stupendous task. An unreformed colonial system of education was simply not up to it. If God were to initiate an inquiry into the poor performance of secularism in India, surely one of the key terms of reference would be why education was not perceived as the central agency for consolidating secularism. Those providing intellectual inputs in the state's enterprise of promoting secularism also showed little interest, and even less insight, in education. You can read whichever author you prefer on this matter, you will find that education is nobody's concern. Of course, each one of them occasionally chants education as a mantra, but its tedious complexity as a means and the details of the task involved in reforming it remain unrecognized, almost as if these are boring matters, suitable for lesser minds to handle. One cannot help saying that the superficiality of educational policy and discussion reveals the colonized character of the secular discourse itself. And from this viewpoint, what India has gone through over the last decade, from Ayodhya to Gujarat, is simply the price paid for a backlog.

In all likelihood the payment will have to continue. As I indicated earlier, the transformative national culture demanded engagement with a varied range of issues, from land reforms to language planning. Education was a key challenge inasmuch as its character would determine whether society could absorb modernity without losing the 'tacit' property of culture (in the sense explained earlier). Both Gandhi and Tagore had worked out models of educational planning which emphasized the tacit aspect of learning. Gandhi's model suggested the use of crafts for this; Tagore's model featured an aesthetic core. Instead of trying to synthesize the two, national policy ignored both, and from the mid-1960s (the turning point being the report of the Kothari Commission)[6] candidly advocated a book-centred approach to school teaching. Not just Gandhi and Tagore, other philosophical resources too, such as Sri Aurobindo and Krishnamurti, were ignored.

Those in charge of educational planning appeared to have no interest in, or patience for, the philosophical basis of education. For them, education was a crude instrument of nation building, and nation building itself meant what Tagore would have called the cultivation of a national ego. By the early 1980s it was clear that education, like radio and television, was of concern to the state merely as a means of propaganda. And we know all too well by now that propaganda was needed in plenty, to hide India's national failure on the welfare front and to highlight its irreversible march towards becoming a nuclear power. The

---

[6] For a discussion of this turning point, see Krishna Kumar, 'Agricultural Modernisation and Education: Contours of a Point of Departure', *Economic and Political Weekly*, 31 (35–7), 1996, pp. 2367–73. The Kothari Commission report was written during 1964–6.

memory of a *nirmanadhin* national culture was finally fading and militaristic nationalism, by definition devoid of any creative principle, was taking over.

There is historical irony in this development. Of the two national projects born during Partition, the Indian project claimed to be more imaginative because it repudiated, and not just shunned, the application of religion as a binding force. As a new nation, Pakistan was based precisely on that applicability of religion, but soon enough it slipped into using religion to cover the state's failure to provide welfare to the people and its own capitulation to global imperialism. It is a strange fact of our times that Pakistan's religio-militaristic nationalism is setting the tone for us, rather than Indian nationalism—ith its promise of democratic social change serving as an inspiration for Pakistan.[7] Both neglected educational reform, permitting their poverty of historical common sense to be perpetuated by a ramshackle system of school education fit only for use as a propaganda machine.

In India, some of us are inconsolably pained these days because our propaganda machine has been stolen by those who have an altogether different script to propagate. In this moment of grief, it is easy for us to overlook the pathetic state of our system of education, irrespective of the shoddy and vicious sense of history that is about to be dispersed through it. Culture and history are among the most sensitive areas of learning because, while dealing with them, schools must engage with the child's socialization at home. All colonial systems of education have the tendency to isolate the child at school from the living reality of daily practices witnessed at home. Curricular arrangements reflecting this tendency benefit from superficial training of teachers, their low economic

---

[7] For an understanding of the complex interlocking of Indo-Pak memories and perceptions, and for a comparative study of the textbooks of history, the children of the two countries are required to read my *Prejudice and Pride*, Viking/Penguin, New Delhi, 2001.

status, and the predominance of prescribed textbooks and centralized examinations. By overlooking this inner world of education, Indian state planners permitted the penetration of schools by ideological forces inimical to the Constitution and its intellectual heritage. In Pakistan, the post-colonial state compromised with religious revivalists all too soon, allowing what little liberal substance the colonial dispensation had to die out.

The two national trajectories differ, but their points of arrival are remarkably similar. It is all too clear that South Asia is now a ready-to-use battleground for two matched militaristic nationalisms. Notwithstanding the fact that India is still a functioning democracy and Pakistan has failed to become one, they both have joined the list of the world's biggest buyers of modern, sophisticated weapons. And, of course, they are both proud owners of nuclear weapons of mass destruction. As inheritors of what undoubtedly was the greatest national movement in the entire colonial world, they both owe an explanation to the world. The explanation must come in two parts: One, how did they fritter away the moral legacy of the freedom struggle? And two, how did they end up becoming a major threat to world peace and potential perpetrators of regional suicide?

11

Understanding Women

The news that women took part in Gujarat's riots does not surprise me. In the middle of a dexterously engineered breakdown of civil society, we cannot expect women will stay aloof from the ethos. However, the scale and nature of their participation in the riots deserves special contemplation at this point in the history of religious separatism in India. My experience of working with young people of both sexes persuades me to believe that communalism, like other political ideologies, has a more nuanced meaning for the girls who believe in it. That it can be discussed with them in a richer context of issues, both social and personal, may have to do with the fact that as of now there are no organizations which target girls at an early age as a specific audience for socialization into a communal outlook. Given the tendencies gaining dominance in our times, such organizations may soon come up or existing ones may take up the vitiation of girls' minds as an added agenda.

If that happens, it will mark an astonishing turn in the short history of women's education and training for civic life in India. This history had its modest beginnings in the last quarter of the nineteenth century. Education played a key role in the radical widening of the range of roles available to women in our society. Between 1875 and 1930, Indian women had altered the social landscape beyond recognition by using institutionalized education as an instrument. True, this happened mainly in the rimland—spanning Bengal, Tamil Nadu, and Maharashtra—and primarily in the upper layers of society, but the impact was dynamic. Though I knew these historical facts, I went through an electrifying experience when I saw the faces of India's early women graduates, doctors, lawyers, nurses, and teachers at an exhibition of photographs held in December. Those faces conveyed a historically new spontaneity. The dresses, the postures, and the gaze of these young women announced the arrival of a new and catalytic agent in India's social chemistry.

From childhood to maturity, and from family to politics, this exhibition covered a remarkable range of contexts and roles. The earliest photographs, taken in the 1870s, were of couples and families, carrying explicit markings of the reluctant joy that the prospect of a permanent record of oneself implied. The preparation one went through before sitting in front of the camera was among the earliest expressions of the modern idea that a woman mattered as an individual, and not just because of the role she played in the family. It is bewildering to think how pervasive a change this idea brought about in the aspirations women could nurture. And if one thinks of the impact the idea had on the institutional fabric of society, one can only term it as revolutionary. There is little doubt that we are still in the middle of that revolution though a lot keeps happening to distract us from noticing its momentous scale. Perhaps it is true that the message that the faces of those early women graduates beamed has not been fully received by men. Translated into words, the message was: 'I know you don't expect to see me like this, but this is the way I'm going to be now.'

Many parts of India continue to be in a chronic state of resistance to women's emancipation, trying to reject or wish away that message. The sight of a girl on her way to school or college is now common, but it continues to arouse an everyday kind of censure and aggression. One of the most chilling incidents to have occurred in India in the recent past was the crushing of a girl inside the gates of her college in Sarguja, by jeep-riding youth to whom she had spoken sternly on being teased. In the Hindi heartland, explicit or tacit violence against girls and women is a daily phenomenon. Of course, domestic violence is not confined to the north, but men's behaviour towards women unrelated to them is quite unique in these parts. In both small towns and cities, a lot of men behave as if they have never seen a woman in their life. It is not surprising, though it was disappointing, that the exhibition had virtually no photographs from the Hindi belt.

For me the most moving part of the exhibition was the special niche where Pandita Ramabai was commemorated. Having recently carried out a study of the portrayal of the freedom struggle in school textbooks, I am acutely aware of the negligible place women have been given in the pantheon of nationalism. Apparently, women have little relevance in the narrow view of nationalism taken by several of our school historians. This is why even a personality as tall as Pandita Ramabai fails to find a significant mention in the grand narrative of nationalism and modernity crafted for the young. Customarily labelled as a social reformer, she was herself a photographer, and some of the pictures she took were displayed at the exhibition. Two of these pictures show the difference that the security and education given to an orphan girl at Ramabai's own institution made to the girl's personality. Ramabai's own face stared resolutely at the exhibition in an allegory of contentment and anger over women's experiences over a century of tension and resolve.

No male viewer could possibly go out of that hall without feeling a little lost. Photograph exhibitions usually make people feel more confident about their grasp of a theme or subject. The two-dimensional, mechanically accurate image instantly reinforces one's ego, with previously held knowledge made more vivid. At the exhibition organized by the Centre for Women's Development Studies, I felt a little giddy and shaken by the sudden awareness of the incompleteness of my mental world. Like many others, I have held on to the general view that colonial subjugation brought great economic misfortune and cultural obsequiousness for India. Scholars of Dalit history have been pointing out that this perception does not do justice to the emancipatory implications of foreign rule for the downtrodden castes. Women constitute a similar blind spot. We do not know how to accommodate their experience in the narrative of India's rise as a nation-state.

Women's participation in politics was a special aspect of India's struggle for freedom from colonial rule. Gandhi used the struggle for independence as an opportunity to break the taboos surrounding women's involvement in public affairs. It was a long jump which left many territories of home and economic life unattended. Political activism furnished the evidence of sumptuous courage and the desire for equality, but the slow-moving progress of education and its poor quality could hardly sustain these developments. This disbalance continues to haunt us, and it is not surprising that women are faced with a backlash today. The neglect of education, compounded by the rise of communal politics, threatens to destroy the gains made during the middle decades of the twentieth century. One of the many moving images I brought back from the exhibition was that of Kamaladevi Chattopadhyaya auctioning salt at Chowpatee. To update history, we should juxtapose that image from the early 1930s with the picture we recently saw of a mob in Sabarmati Ashram demanding the handing over of Medha Patkar. Terrible and ominous though this juxtaposition looks, it helps us to estimate the challenge Indian women face in the present scenario. Of course they have no alternative. Five generations have passed since they gave up the easier course of living as social clones of men.

12

Adolescent India

When I first saw the word 'Kishore' written on a signboard in the campus of that unique institution, Kishore Bharati, my heart filled up with a vague apprehension. Can the turbulent romanticism and attraction for abstractions associated with being a *kishore* or adolescent be institutionalized? Later on, when Kishore Bharati's amazing world suddenly vanished, it felt as if a dream had ended. Fortunately, Kishore Bharati left behind its more stable progeny, Eklavya, aptly named after the tribal boy who refused to be deterred by the difficulty of finding an accepting teacher and carrying on with archery without a thumb. The challenges before today's tribal adolescents are no less daunting, and the larger context is far more volatile and complex than it was in the times of the Mahabharata.

Why just tribal adolescents, childhood in rural India as a whole is in a state we would rather not appreciate. In the case of infants and children attending the primary classes at school, we know the extent of the neglect they suffer, and therefore can hope for improvement. In the states of the south, the system is in better shape, and might develop new characteristics like imagination and flexible responsiveness. In the rest of India, improvement in the rural child's lot is going to take much more effort than the system in place is ready to put in. But when it comes to the rural adolescent, no one has taken stock of the scale of issues.

Let me first share what little I know about the psychological dimensions of the problem we face. The previous sentence conceals no personal apology. Drawing upon psychology is a genuine problem. Developmental psychologists are a shrinking tribe in India, their language an endangered discourse. I do not meet people who have read the works of the late Durganand Sinha. Sudhir Kakar is now better known as a novelist than for his path-breaking study of male infancy, *The Inner World*.[1] This classic can still frighten and inspire even if you take its message half as seriously as it is conveyed in the book. The mother-son continuum Kakar draws in the context of infancy is grounded in a world in which the young mother depends on her son for emotional security. The book explains how this romantic bond sets in a cycle of dependency and fear when infancy terminates, rather dramatically, and a long, confused male latency and adol-escence starts, the latter characterized by the foreknowledge that independence is a futile dream.

I have already gone a little beyond Kakar's balanced description into my own summary of the limited literature we possess on adolescence in modernizing India. One of the key points of this summary is that adolescence in India is marked by confusion over personal and collective identity in addition to the sadness that the sudden end to a prolonged infancy imprints on the growing male. Comparable analysis of the socialization of girls is hard to come by. How girls become women is something we know rather little about, though literary and biographical knowledge is now becoming available.

The family holds the key to containing the fire that muzzled dreaming ignites. The success of development planning in certain parts of India has a great deal to do with the secret, unsolicited cooperation that the state has received from the

---

[1] Oxford University Press, New Delhi, 1982.

family. Trouble has begun to brew because the family appears to be losing its grip. The millions of infants who grow up with an absentee father or who have no memories of a stable dwelling have an orientation to life no one can delineate offhand. There are many parts of metropolitan India where the alienation of adolescents and youth matches descriptions generated in the metropolitan slums of Latin America and Africa. Unemployment has been steadily rising in the countryside; the institution which has permitted the state the luxury of neglecting the rise is the family. How far can the family serve this role?

In the absence of decent sociological studies from different parts of the country, one leans on literature, personal knowledge of those who know better, and logical deduction. These are not reliable indicators of anything, but they do have suggestive value. It seems the family, particularly the authority of the father in enforcing decisions, is still strong, but the more generalized hold of the family in shaping urges and conduct is waning. Neither the immediate nor the distant context is conducive to the family's capacity to socialize the young for a life of uncertainty and the force of unknown factors.

The spread of small arms across the northern countryside has cast an everyday shadow of violence. The spread of television has routinized a culture of sensations which are not capable of being translated from the virtual to the physical world. As an experience, education has failed to gain respect in the village though it has acquired status. It is not associated in the popular mind with ideas or lasting inner resources, but only with opportunities to earn money, and these opportunities are scarce even in the urban world, what to speak of the village. The implication is an unpurposive, rather depressive youth culture.

How pervasive it is may be hard to assess, but there is continuity between stampede deaths in a UP town when an army recruitment drive attracts a few lakhs, and deaths in India's software capital following the passing away of a matinee hero.

One of the many roles education performs as a matter of routine is to declare several million youngsters 'fail'. Both in scale and in its dramatic character, this annual labelling exercise can only be compared to the inoculation programme, the only difficulty in this comparison being that the award of 'fail' status enhances the receiver's vulnerability whereas inoculation imparts protection. What happens to the stigmatized? Those who get categorized as failures within a school stage mostly drag on, hoping to 'pass' next summer. The official expression 'retention' is a matter of policy—although state practices vary— in the primary classes, hence those who fail cannot easily disenrol. However, those who fail in the final year of a stage, for example, in grades five, eight, or ten, have a strong chance of not coming back.

I have often wondered why failing is treated as an active verb in the English grammar. In Hindi it is not possible to attribute failure directly to the one who has failed—*woh fail ho gaya*, the 'ho' suggesting external forces. In public lore, however, the word conveys hubris. The one who fails at school carries not just a stigma but also a sense of fate.

For a long time, failure at college carried a form of residual prestige, derived from having gone to college and having appeared at a university exam. In her study of autobiographies written by Indians during the nineteenth and early twentieth centuries, Judith Walsh records the popularity of the letterhead entry 'BA Fail'. Universities like Calcutta flaunted their high failure rate as a means of conveying rigour. Calcutta still takes pride in being stingy about awarding a first class which stands at 60 per cent. School boards have now increasingly made this a redundant watershed; in Delhi, for instance, a 60 per cent scorer has no hope of admission to a course or college of choice.

Despite the inflation in high school scores, the idea that a high rate of failure means a better exam continues to sit peacefully in the public mind, muddy and bewildered though it is on account of familiar stories of exam culture, such as mass copying, contracted centres, proxy candidates, and so on. Generally, it seems the newspaper reading public feels reassured when the pass percentage is low. Such sordid stuff is for villagers to cope with. The fact that the Central Board of Secondary Education (CBSE) results—announced in the Delhi media as if they are national results—show a high pass percentage in 'public' schools merely confirms the popular perception of these schools as being decent institutions. Provincial boards do not have the aura of CBSE; their pass percentages are not widely known. Tenth grade results are typically far lower than grade twelve, which is in all likelihood a structural feature of the system. It permits the system to siphon off a few million children after the tenth grade. What happens to them?

When people like 'us', that is, educated, successful, and upwardly mobile, think of career options for our children, we have in mind certain kinds of trajectories all of which end up in living a copy of what is regarded as a decent life. We have been vaguely aware since our childhoods that this kind of lifestyle is not available to all, that it cannot become available to all. Some of us recognize, if the earth is to be saved, that the lifestyle of the effectively educated need not be available to all. When we were young, it was accessible to just a few families in the district. Thousands of others who lived in the town headquarters and the vast countryside surrounding it lived a different life cycle, with no bank accounts, no admission forms, no Value Payable Post (VPP) deliveries from shops located in distant cities.

The great development game aimed at stretching the orbit of this lifestyle, with saving accounts in post offices, fertilizers and functional literacy. Now, some forty years after bank nationalization and the arrival of foreign banks, and hybrid seeds which brought the Green Revolution giving way to genetically modified seeds, 'we' feel the country has bypassed the worst fallouts of what was described in books that our fathers read as explosion of the population bomb. Little do we realize, and our morning papers shield us from any thought that might invade and offer the insight, that the countryside is exploding with rampant unemployment, displacement, violence, and a sense of hopelessness among adolescents.

Adolescents are supposed to be especially prone to the depression of the idealistic, not the depression of the bewildered and the frustrated. To offer hope to our rural adolescents of both sexes, we must try to understand what happens to the dreams they are supposed to entertain in the course of their natural development as young adults. These dreams are often vague, at least partly because the kind of education rural schools provide fails to nurture self-worth and the capacity to reflect on oneself. Language teaching is dominated by the anxiety to mainstream, denying dignity to rural tongues, ignoring the role that language plays in building memory and imagination.

Any positive planning for the rural adolescent must take into account what is happening in the context of agriculture and in the heritage craft sectors. These two are our civilizational resources, and it is wrong to see them in purely material terms. Biotechnology is undoubtedly an exciting field to those of us who regard the pursuit of it as something good for its own sake, but its meaning for the peasant who will negotiate his own and his family's existence in the shadow of a world he will decipher even less than he deciphered the inscription on pesticide bottles is quite different.

If I go on in this vein, I will lose quite a few of my readers, especially those who work as civil servants and are excited by the tiny fruits and seeds of post-industrial development that have been showered on India of late. They do not want to engage with issues that complicate development plans already in place. I wonder if they have accepted the prospect of a vast death for India's rural masses, in the battle for sustainable modernity for the India that has begun to look like a pale copy of the smaller countries of Europe.

If I am wrong, I would like to make a plea in defence of some conventional ideas and institutions. Decent schooling and health at the public expense of the state are primarily qualifiers for the title of a welfare state. Let us not outsource these; let us not destroy the institutional apparatus that was devised in the Nehru era to strive for these basic services. The apparatus, even the Directorate of Education, deserves to be reformed, not destroyed, in the name of privatization or panchayati raj. Good governance must be inclusive, giving a place to all players, but someone has to take responsibility.

It is nobody's design that our state secretariats and directorates of education are preoccupied with transfers and court cases. These offices of Victoria's raj need curriculum experts, professional managers of mass recruitment and publication, psychologists, sociologists, and artists to guide policy. Each school needs counsellors and curriculum consultants, telephones and Internet, a library and workshop. Enrichment of the rural school will create, apart from lakhs of jobs and business opportunities, an ethos capable of inspiring the young to succeed in a million different ways rather than fail in just one.

All this and more can be planned and done if we stop dreaming like adolescents and sit up like adults to take a realistic look at our stunted, bruised system. If the village school is to be upgraded and improved, the headmaster and teachers would need better salary and status, not worse than what it is. It is simply amazing how rigid and cold our provincial directorates and district-level authorities are towards teachers. Casualization of the teaching workforce in the name of accountability will decimate a role that has given inspiration and reason to hope to millions of youth. On areas linked to education and livelihoods, craft cooperatives will need to be nourished as economic and pedagogic bodies. DIETs will require an apparatus capable of serving the curricular needs of schools, and for this industrialists will need to help.

An Institute of Education in every district was not a bad starting point, but we have made little progress in giving imaginative functions to this institute. In general, the bureaucracy has managed to keep new institutions like the DIET under tight control of the kind that schools have been used to. Imparting of authority and a professional leadership role to school heads can help us move on. This calls for a policy to treat the school as a unit, open them up to civic intervention, and to recognize teaching as an inviolable professional activity (as suggested by the Chattopadhyay Commission). I suppose the satisfaction of running one Navodaya in every district is so great that we do not want to even imagine what it might mean to run every school like a Navodaya, or at least like a Kendriya Vidyalaya. Children born in families of central government servants have enjoyed the KVs' modest, decent national norms. When will it be time to say that India is capable of extending these norms to schools whose children did not organize their birth so it would occur in a central government servant's home?

13

The New Politics of Education

The conceptual revolution implied in the verdict delivered by the Supreme Court in October 2002 in what is popularly known as the minorities case (TMA Pai Foundation vs State of Karnataka) has been stemmed for the time being; or, to use judicial language, 'clarified' by a constitutional bench headed by Justice V.N. Khare (Islamic Academy of Education vs State of Karnataka, 2003). The earlier verdict, delivered as the majority view by an eleven-judge bench headed by Justice B.N. Kirpal, dealt with questions which had arisen and accumulated over the years regarding the special educational rights given by the Constitution to religious and linguistic minorities. The judgement responded to these questions by first framing them in the state's relationship with private enterprise in education. This is where the verdict's revolutionary implications—temporarily moderated by Justice Khare's review—come from. The term 'revolutionary' calls for an explanation, for it is commonly used to suggest a push towards egalitarian redistribution of educational opportunities under the state's leadership. If the conceptual shift indicated by Justice Kirpal's verdict is viewed from the perspective of the value-premises of the Constitution— at least insofar as these premises were understood up until the verdict arrived—one would be hard-pressed to call it counter-revolutionary. It may be a matter of debate whether the Constitution was intended to be adequately equipped to control the privatization of education, or, alternatively, to promote it. The debate may extend to the evolutionary nature of the state and its relation to the market. Important though this debate is, it need not stop us from noticing that the judicial decoding of the Constitution's intent seems to have changed direction over the last two decades or so. Inquiry into this possibility is as important as the larger, more theoretical study, of whether the Constitution was futuristic enough in designing state–market relations in education.

Three major verdicts given by the Supreme Court during the 1980s and the 1990s goaded the state to assume greater responsibility and show more urgency than it had done in the past in the matter of providing access to education. These verdicts (Bandhua Mukti Morcha vs the Union of India, 1981; Mohini Jain vs Karnataka State,1992; Unnikrishnan vs Andhra Pradesh, 1993) seemed to offer eminent examples of the hermeneutic space available in the Constitution, revealing how important it was to read the Constitution imaginatively in order to crystallize the ideas that may not have been fully articulated. The crowning exercise of this kind figured in the Mohini Jain case in which, though the petitioner got no relief, the court extended the scope of Article 21 by reading into the fundamental right to life a vision of life worth living which would include the nurturing force of education during childhood. This hermeneutic exercise was widely hailed as a major advance in the evolution of democratic polity. It was expected that the court's interpretation of Article 21 would trigger significant civil activism on behalf of the educationally deprived. This expectation was not fulfilled as such, but after what one may call a gestation period—spread over several years spent drafting and nearly one full year at the end taken on account of correctness of dating—it led to the enactment of an amendment in the Constitution which rendered elementary education an explicitly stated fundamental right.

This important legislative and legal event has, however, failed to round off debates concerning fundamental issues on which our concepts of education and childhood depend. The new right granted to children leaves the state free to impart education by any means that it may by law determine to be suitable for this purpose. This freedom arouses appreciable suspicion, considering the history of the reluctance among policy-makers to pin the state down to a commitment to promising every child the opportunity to study at a school. The 1986 policy treated non-formal education as a valid alternative to schooling, and during the recent years we have witnessed the official acceptance of several other alternative modes. Clearly, neither the court nor the parliament have succeeded in making a dent on the systemic tendency to first devise a cheaper alternative for the poor and then to promise populist measures to improve it. It has been argued[1] that the constitutional amendment has created a situation worse than what prevailed following the Supreme Courts verdicts in the cases of Mohini Jain and Unni-krishnan. The difference between the two situations is, of course, only of a notional nature because neither the court nor the parliament could be expected to change the system and the tendencies inherent in it by one-time action. In the absence of systemic reform, one cannot hope for clearer perception or stronger will to counter the ideology which permits childhood to be defined differently for the labouring poor from how is defined for the well-off. This ideology is also at the heart of the other debate which concerns pre-school years. The state's responsibility towards these precious, formative years of life has been suitably accommodated in the amended version of the same Article 45 which had served little use to achieve the purpose stated in it and which, therefore, required the enhancement of Article 21.

[1] For example, see Anil Sadgopal, 'Political Economy of the Ninety-Third Amendment Bill', *Mainstream*, 22 December 2001, pp. 43–9.

While this exercise of devising safe strategies of law-making were underway, the judiciary went ahead to read further meanings in the provisions of the Constitution, but in this round the reading has been of a different kind. During 2002, two cases gave occasion for such an exercise, one being the curriculum cases (Aruna Roy vs Union of India) and the other was the minorities case. In the first, the court upheld the NCERT's National Curriculum Framework and its intention to inculcate values through education by using religion as a resource. The verdict said that a religion-based strategy for value education is not incompatible with the spirit of secularism so long as vigilance is exercised in order to ensure that the strategy does not slip into indoctrination. In the second case, the court's verdict depends more substantially on the hermeneutic challenge of deciding what all the freedom to pursue an occupation granted under Article 19 (g) entails. The majority judgement given by Justice Kirpal perceives in this right the scope to allow all citizens to establish educational institutions of their choice. Even if there is any doubt about whether education is a profession or not, it does appear that education will fall within the meaning of the expression 'occupation', says the verdict, apparently and perhaps inadvertently, stretching the most visible activity associated with education, namely, teaching, to include the enterprise of the setting up of an institution where teachers are hired. The verdict uses this window of interpretive opportunity to endow legitimacy to institutions established by members or bodies of the majority religious community. The structure of the argument suggests that the scope of private initiative in education has been read so liberally, that is, through a fundamental right so unobjectionable as the right to pursue an occupation, in order to extend the boundaries of the right of educational enterprises and autonomy so far restricted to religious minorities. For arriving at this decision, Justice Kripal read Article 19.1 (g) in juxtaposition with Article 26. The former grants the right to carry on any occupation, and the latter imparts to all citizens belonging to any religious denomination or its sections the freedom to establish and maintain institutions for 'religious or charitable purposes'. The argument pursued in the verdict highlights the essentially charitable nature of educational activity in order to assign to all religious communities the right to establish educational institutions. Presumably, these will qualify to be called 'private' institutions.

Two equally important issues are intertwined in this argument. One pertains to the educational rights of religious minorities in comparison to the majority; the other concerns the freedom available to private, unaided institutions. On the first of these issues the five-member bench led by Justice Khare has given a significant clarification. According to it, the right given by Justice Kirpal's verdict to the majority community is not on par with the right given specifically by the Constitution to religious minorities. Why this should be so is explained by invoking the extreme situation in which the state decides to nationalize all private institutions. Even in that extreme scenario, the clarification says, minority institutions will stand protected because of the special provision of Article 30. This clarification is undoubtedly a source of great relief under the prevailing circumstances, but we can easily see in the methodology of the extreme-case scenario the difficulty that the five-member bench probably faced, attempting to locate any viable discursive space to keep minority rights somewhat above or distinct from the common right the earlier verdict by Justice Kirpal had given to all religious denominations under the broad banner of freedom of occupation. The extreme-case-scenario as a method of reasoning is, of course, valid, but in the given circumstances created by Justice Kirpal's verdict, the use of this method of reasoning presents grim apprehensions. Nationalization of private institutions on account of being private, and in that sense autonomous, looks an unlikely event, given the speed at which privatization is growing and gaining legitimacy, and not from Justice Kirpal's verdict. But nationalization on account of rampant use of education for majoritarian indoctrination cannot be viewed as an altogether exotic happening in the foreseeable future, assuming that political forces opposed to such indoctrination will have the strength to gain the time required to check the process by drastic state intervention.

Justice Kirpal's verdict has a substantial section devoted to the appreciation of private enterprise in education. The verdict links private initiative with quality and defines the latter in terms of facilities, including infrastructure and teachers. It is not self-evident why the verdict goes at such length into this discussion, for it has been nobody's plea that private initiative in education should be discouraged or checked. The question before the court was 'whether there can be government regulation, and if so, to what extent'. In answer to this question, Justice Kirpal's verdict eulogizes private education as 'one of the most dynamic and fastest growing segments of post-secondary education for which a combination of circumstances and the inability or unwillingness of government to provide the necessary support' are responsible. As the discussion proceeds, the possibility pointing to the state's 'unwillingness' is dropped, only the 'inability' remains, permitting the construction of the need to regulate or restrain the state from interfering in the running of private institutions. The verdict makes a reference to 'the logic of economics and the ideology of privatisation' as having contributed to the resurgence of private higher education. Later, the verdict makes a case for treating autonomy as the highest value of private education.

This point is reinforced with a citation from the Radhakrishnan Commission of 1948 in which the exclusive control of education by the state was viewed as a facilitator of 'totalitarian tyrannies'. This citation is used as a basis for cautioning against the government's attempt to interfere in the running of unaided institutions by nominating specific individuals on governing bodies, in appointment of teachers and admission of students, and in the shaping of the fee structure. In all these matters, the verdict expects the private institutions to follow reasonable policies rather than let 'bureaucratic or government interference undermine their independence'. Thus, the perceived risk is not that of unaided institutions exploiting the teachers, the students and their parents, but rather that of bureaucratic interference.

A few remarks have also been made about private schools, and these are contextualized with the help of terms like today's 'competitive world' and the role of 'economic forces'. The discussion leaves us with no uncertainty whatsoever that the court wishes to encourage private activity in school education:

The state says that it has no funds to establish institutions of the same level of excellence as private schools. But by curtailing the income of such private schools, it disables these schools from affording the best facilities because of a lack of funds. If this lowering of standards from excellence to a level of mediocrity is to be avoided, the state has to provide the difference, which, therefore, brings us back to a vicious circle to the original problem, viz, the lack of state funds. The only solution would appear to lie in the states not using their scanty resources to prop up institutions that are able to otherwise maintain themselves out of the fees charged, but in improving the facilities and infrastructure of state-run schools and in subsidising the fees payable by the students there. It is in the interest of the general public that more good schools are established, autonomy and non-regulation of the school administration in the right of appointment, admission of the students and the fee to be charged will ensure that more such schools are established.[2]

This argument is essentially an elaboration of the position taken earlier in the verdict that the provision made following the Unnikrishnan case curtails the right of private professional institutions in an unreasonable manner and therefore needs to be reviewed. The provision under question had to do with the state's right to interfere in the admission policy and the fee

[2] *TMA Pai Foundation* v. *State of Karnataka*, 2002. Case No.: Writ Petition (Civil) 317 of 1993.

structure of private professional institutions. The Unnikrishnan case led to the system of two lists, one consisting of the so-called 'free' seats and the other announcing the 'payment' seats. The verdict given by Justice Kirpal found that apart from creating several practical difficulties, this arrangement was also morally indefensible, on the ground that the urban student is likely to have an edge over the rural student, and shall therefore figure in the 'free' list, which would mean that the rural student would subsidize the education of the urban. This is hardly an egalitarian situation, argues the verdict. The cancellation of the Unnikrishnan arrangement, on the basis of the argument given above, created a crisis, necessitating the appointment of Justice Khare's bench for clarification. On the ground that this year's academic session had already begun, the review verdict permits the arrangement in place so far to continue, but here onwards a committee chaired by a high court judge will oversee the mechanisms of state–private management relations.

These practical complexities inherent in the maintenance of a dual system in a society headed for greater divisiveness and politicization of institutions will undoubtedly need further clarification by the court in the years to come despite the comment with which Justice Khare's verdict concludes:

It is unfortunate that a Constitution Bench had to be constituted for interpreting an 11 Judge Bench judgment. In the judicial history of India this has been done for the first time. It is equally unfortunate that all of us cannot agree on all the points, despite the fact that the matter involves construction of a judgment. In the name of interpretation we have to some extent, however little it may be, rewritten the judgment....

The superior courts in India exist for interpretation of the Constitution or interpretation of the statutes. They cannot evolve a foolproof system on the basis of affidavits filed by the parties or upon hearing their counsel. Certain details of vexing problems on the basis of the interpretation given by this court must be undertaken by the statutory bodies which have the requisite expertise. It is expected that statutory bodies would be able to perform their duties for which they

have been established. The doors of the court should not be knocked
every time, if a problem arises in the implementation of the judgment
however slight it may be.[3]

These words ought to occasion some reflection on why statutory
bodies are not doing their job, why other bodies—such as the
Central Advisory Board of Education (CABE), which may not be
statutory but are historically well-established—are not allowed
to function. In the curriculum case, the court did not think that
non-consultation with CABE rendered the NCF unauthorized.
By revisiting its own judgement in the minorities case so soon
after it was delivered and so thoroughly, the honourable court
has expressed its concern and ambivalence on the role and
status of the state as a regulator of educational opportunity. This
ambivalence is characteristic of the response all three pillars
of the state are making to the emerging political economy and
underneath the ambivalence one can read a sense of disbelief
that the world has changed as much as it apparently has. As
for the academia, it does seem to possess a vague recognition
that the coming years will bring unfamiliar challenges to the
concept and maintenance of higher education as a system. That
the challenges could be grim, posing the question of survival
to large parts of the higher education system in the country
is not yet perceived as an imminent reality. Here too, there is
the same sense of disbelief and ambivalence that the judiciary
has displayed. The general ethos continues to be in favour of
discrediting alarmist discourses in the name of maintaining
academic integrity. Indeed, alarmists are typified as people who
have taken a position and who are not willing to engage with
reality. The idea that India needs rapid expansion of its school
system and excellence in its higher education is believed to be
now so simple a priority that any attempt to analyse things is

[3] *Islamic Academy of Education* v. *State of Karnataka*, 2003. Case
No.: Writ Petition (Civil) 350 of 1993.

held up as a waste of time if not as a conspiracy to impede the nation's progress.

It is in this kind of emergency that privatization is galloping forward both at the school and higher levels and the state has proved incapable of regulating this phenomenon. A whole new culture of schooling is taking shape, leaving the Doon School model of privileged education looking like a memento of obsolete nationalism. The new private schools now advertise facilities which are identical to those offered by five-star hotels, and the management practices followed in the two are similar. Many of these schools are run by non-resident Indians (NRIs) who make it appear as if they are inspired by a sense of duty towards the country of their origin and their concern for its potential for competing in the global market. Few analysts notice any specific politics in the NRI's interest in India, and quite a few innocently link it with the vague discourse of globalization. Busy as social researchers are studying the poor, no one devotes attention to studying the rich non-residents and their local agents. The new trend among the schools of the wealthy is to affiliate for certification with global bodies like the International Baccalaureate. Though physically located right next to metropolitan cities, in suburbs or on highways, there is little knowledge available on how they run, what they offer, and what they imply for the system of education in India. Here is a description of one such school:

The day, week and full-boarding system make the school unique in character. The especially designed residences separate for boys and girls are centrally air-conditioned with every conceivable facility in order to provide more home like and fully secure environment to about 500 boarders. Excellent food is served while maintaining a high standard of cleanliness, hygiene and a well-balanced diet.

The school has facilities like multipurpose hall, swimming pool, preparatory rooms, playpen for kids, music and dance rooms, arts and crafts room, counselling room, well-laid out staff quarters, sports complex, offering facilities for the usual sports plus horse-riding and golf. And then, there is a fleet of 16 air-conditioned luxury coaches with attendants and mobile phones.[4]

All this must, at one level, sound laughable, and some might even regard it as being worthy of being laughed away; yet, the sketch also serves as a measure of the upper limits to which the notion of facilities can extend. This would be an important measure for a society where the highest judicial institution sees nothing wrong with facilities being treated as an indication of quality. Seasoned administrators of education and NGOs working for the education of the poor or for the eradication of child labour might well ask why they should bother about schools the super-rich are running for their children if the state is not involved. This conceptualization of the state treats it as being an outsider to the society in which it is supposed to function, as a kind of adjunct designed to look after those who cannot look after themselves. How a state conceptualized so trivially can develop a vision or policy of education is anybody's guess. The concept of education sustaining different national systems for more than a century is inextricably intertwined with the concept of the modern state. The speedy re-mapping of state–market relations that is occurring across the world has grim implications for the concept of public education as a state responsibility. The late Basil Bernstein (1996) wrote that 'the principles of the market and its managers are more and more the managers of the policies and the practices of education'.[5] The phenomenon Bernstein is referring to has gained remarkable acceleration in India over the decade of the 1990s, but it remains largely undocumented and uninterpreted, thanks to the common assumption that privatization is occurring on

[4] 'Birth of a Star', in Living Legends, *The Indian Express* (space marketing feature), October, 2003, p. 11.

[5] *Pedagogy, Symbolic Control and Identity*, Taylore and Francis, London, 1996.

the fringes of the mainstream. Interestingly, market forces are also clueless and disorganized, merely responding to a range of opportunities arising out of the sharpening social divisions and inequalities. The popular view that private control promises quality—and this view now has the Supreme Court's concurrence—is helping to sustain the ethos in which private interests can boldly advance and the state withdraws.

Both in the national space and globally, education is now acquiring recognition as a key instrument of domination in the face of demo-cratic upsurge. Even as the discourse of education as empowerment and liberation continues to occupy centre stage in state rhetoric, shared by NGOs and international bodies, the potential that education offers as a means of legitimizing exclusion and oppression is being tested on a scale way ahead of what research can keep up with. The new super-schools are acquiring the character of export zones of industrial production where any normative supervision by law is perceived as bureaucratic intrusion which is harmful for the pursuit of quality and maintenance of the competitive edge. We can hypothesize that this mutated concept of institutionalized education will resuscitate old institutions such as caste and race, which had begun to look weak, even defunct, to many. Religion had never fully withdrawn from the modern educational space, even in the highly industrialized countries where modernity is supposed to have made its deepest dent; and now we are already witnessing a significant rise in support of religious education in schools. This is the real context of the new interpretation of the Constitution under which the majority religious community will have as much right to start private educational institutions as the minorities have. The privilege given to the latter is no more a concession indicating the national awareness that minorities might feel culturally insecure. Withdrawal of the taboo on the majority religious community enjoying a similar privilege indicates that the state's secular ideals can no more be regarded as a matter of national faith. This is a major dissolution persuading us to recognize that India is being reinvented.[6] But, of course, it is not just India that is being reinvented. Even as we ponder on the process—asking closely whether it is a process or a project—we need to guard against the wholesale sacrifice of the humanist concept of education for a cold, instrumentalist substitute which promises quality control by focusing on outcomes, both pedagogic and social. Under the new concept, universal literacy will ensure that women's fertility is controlled, the masses are socialized for brief, just-in-time jobs and scared submission to the regime of capital, and the elite are persuaded to shed liberal ambivalence over the frequent use of force for the maintenance of order.

---

[6] S. Corbridge and J. Harris, *Reinventing India*, Oxford University Press, New Delhi, 2000.

14

Computers and Children

Parents and teachers don't believe you if you tell them that computers do little good to children. Aren't American and European pre-schools already fitted with computers? If they are, then there must be something good about exposing children to the exciting world of computers at an early age. And also, if computers are going to pervade our lives in the years to come, isn't it a good idea to get children used to them early? Computers are not just machines, you are told; they are symbols of human transformation. So, why shouldn't children gain mastery over them before starting their journey of life?

Why not, indeed? Educational theorists worldwide are not yet convinced about the good that computers might do during childhood. David Elkind, an American expert on children's learning, has this to say about the argument that computers can assist in children's mental development:

With succeeding generations of computer language, even young children may be able to interact with computers in ways that would permit reflective abstraction. But we are not there yet, and for the present, computers that present programmed learning to young children are examples of miseducation.[1]

----

[1] *Miseducation: Preschoolers at Risk*, Knopf, New York, 1987.

Elkind is guarded because the idea that computers may have negative consequences for childhood could made him seem out of his mind.

And yet, it is easy to appreciate the dilemma that anyone who knows either children or pedagogy well would face if asked about the merit of introducing computers in children's education. Exciting though the interactive potential of learning with the help of a computer is, such learning is no substitute for interacting with the environment and the objects in it. Computers have an addictive effect, but even if one might protect children against such an effect by monitoring the hours they spend with it (see how successful we have been in preventing similar addiction of TV!), we cannot compare the experience of unguided play or the pursuit of an interest in nature with the experience of sitting before a computer. The world of childhood does shrink when knowledge takes the shape of a monitor.

Advocates of computers and educational policy-makers, however, are determined to treat computers as isolated symbols of progress and modernization. That is why, schools which have no clean toilets or drinking water, nor decent libraries and laboratories, are being equipped with computers. A dingy, crumbling structure with one air-conditioned room where the computer sits could well become a symbol of good school education under budget constraints. There is no sign that educational priorities have a chance of acceptance across all the states. Symbolic gestures are all we usually get in the name of priorities. The *Saraswati Vandana* and computers are examples of such symbolic gestures. Neither is going to mean restructuring and consolidation of our sad, struggling system.

Maybe we will start rethinking the illusory promise of the infotech industry when Western educators begin to question it openly. The fact is that not just questioning but even resistance has already begun. In his book, *The Digital Diploma Mills*,[2] David

---

[2] Monthly Review Press, New York, 2002.

Noble unveils the sordid face of corporate interests who are promoting online education with the collaboration of university administrations and governments. Their primary motive is to bring the faculty under disciplinary control, then to de-skill it, and finally to dispense with it. As Noble says, 'Once the faculty convert their courses to courseware, their services are, in the long run, no longer needed.'

A common plea one hears these days is that students love hi-tech instruction. In at least two major American universities, students have voted against hi-tech instruction, and this kind of resistance is growing. A new movement, reasserting the role of the university as a source of free thought and enquiry based on face-to-face relationships has begun to take shape. Our trajectory in India may be a little different, but we can be rest assured that the assertion of teachers' autonomy will soon come in conflict with the forces of commercialization in education, both hi-tech and others.

15

Colour of a Girl's Skin

Nelson Mandela's 90th birthday received scant attention in India, which was not all that surprising, given how big a country we are and how many events crowd our daily national life. A birthday ignored is hardly a major oversight but this one seems to signify a deeper reality waiting to be explored. As a nation-state, India has consistently opposed prejudice against dark skin and any kind of colour-based discrimination. The significance of its stand acquired personal meaning for me during a visit to Cape Town two years ago when I got the opportunity to visit Robben Island. The solitary prison cell in which Mr. Mandela spent 18 years (out of his 27 years in jail) is located there. A fellow prisoner was escorting our group, led by D. Purandeshwari, the then Minister of State for Human Resource Development. Like many prisoners including Mr. Mandela, our guide was also forced to work in a lime quarry in the blinding sun for many years, irreparably damaging his eyes. He kept his thick black glasses on throughout the tour, even inside buildings. Driving and walking across the island, with its stunted trees and haunted, desolate structures, left us both numbed and agitated. When the visit was about to end, he told the Minister that he wanted a picture taken with her. He said he had never met anyone representing the Indian government which had boldly opposed the West-supported apartheid regime in South Africa. He wanted to convey his thanks to the Indians. Our eyes welled up when he stood beside the Minister to get his picture taken.

A story by Hindi journalist Bhasha Singh, which appeared last month in the weekly *Outlook* (Hindi) reminded me of the visit to Robben Island. Ms Singh, who specializes in rural reporting, filed this story from the Chaugai village of Aara district in Bihar. The story is about the campaign launched by a company to promote its product, a fairness cream. The company wishes to expand its rural market by wooing rural girls. The bait is that the regular application of the cream will make them look fairer. Ms Singh describes how malnourished, poor girls were learning to draw the digit 8 on their faces with the cream. Saroj, who made a perfect 8 on her forehead, is a Class I dropout. In the next stage of the contest, Saroj and her friends will apply the cream for 28 days after which the company team will judge who looks the fairest. The mothers of these girls are already convinced that getting fairer will be good for their matrimonial prospects. They are, of course, right. In the narrow universe shaped by patriarchy and poverty, there are no goals in a girl's life other than marriage and motherhood. It is easy to demolish what little self-esteem they might have been left with, after being aborted by the school without any gains made. Colour of the skin is a well-chosen subject to mobilize them to look for a remedy if there is one. Rural girls constitute a vast market which presents no behavioural resistance, nor does it offer any specific ethical or legal barrier. Market strategists of the fairness cream have realized that it is best to catch their potential consumers young—before rational priorities such as health and nutrition stake claim on their minds.

There are several issues worth worrying about in this scenario. Let us begin with child rights, an idea which has hardly any meaning for girls in general and rural girls in particular. Compared to boys, the lives which Indian girls are taught to perceive as normal include routine discrimination and oppression from early childhood. No right is more basic than the right to be born rather than be killed because you are going to be a female. The rapid growth of female foeticide tells us how far away India has moved from its Constitution's vision of gender equality.

In a collection of research studies on female foeticide edited by Tulsi Patel, eminent demographer Ashish Bose has called the phenomenon a signifier of 'civilizational collapse.' The most depressing aspect of Tulsi Patel's volume is the evidence it provides us to appreciate that the growth of female foeticide is linked to rising literacy, prosperity and modernization, not poverty and backwardness. Apparently, the project of modernity has gone seriously astray if we assess it in the context of girls. The spread of literacy and education has failed to bring about the expected change in their lives because the negative forces of tradition and ritual which shape the larger social ethos have hardened. The economics of consumerism and the politics of identity have together encouraged the misogyny deeply rooted in the social ethos. The campaign by the fairness cream manufacturer to expand its rural market needs to be seen in this wider context. The private sector is now perceived as a partner in development but it stays beyond civil society's ethical scrutiny. It is impervious to legal instruments such as the Right to Information Act designed to make the state answerable. We cannot use our right to information to find out the scale of the promotional activity, of which Ms Singh gave us a glimpse in her report. But I wonder why we cannot expect the government of Bihar to assess the damage being done to the self-esteem of rural girls who are being told to look fairer. The chances of our expectation being fulfilled, are, of course, dim, considering the enormity of the challenges Bihar faces in reforming governance. But the question is not confined to Bihar. The company's relentless campaign to promote its skin whitening cream knows no geographical or national boundaries. It targets girls and women as a species whose human right to be accepted and treated with dignity is yet to be realized.

Scholars like Aneel Kirmani of the University of Michigan have critically looked at the campaign from the point of view of business ethics, and others have found sufficient evidence of potentially toxic physiological effects. But none of this matters in the brave new world of global capital itching to penetrate every nook and cranny of rural Asia and Africa. Let us remember the history of the promotion of formula milk which killed millions of babies in Africa. The case of the fairness cream is different but worse, for it impedes the historic possibility of women's empowerment and the social transformation it would imply. The conundrum of India's warm support to the anti-apartheid politics of Mr. Mandela and prejudice against dark skin stands resolved. We appear to be a nation which has no colour bias as such, and there are no legal cases involving colour-based discrimination. Although matrimonial columns in newspapers are rife with demands for fair skin, no one will accept that India is a colour-conscious nation. The reason we do not perceive ourselves as a colour-conscious nation is that our distaste for dark skin expresses itself only in the context of girls and women—an already subjugated category. Unlike a boy, a dark girl needs substantial compensation to compete in the marriage market. Since women's domestication is a 'given', and neither the spread of education nor economic development of a region makes it different, we don't allow our attitudes towards women to interfere with our general vision of ourselves as a nation. In a man's world, India has no great reason or urgency to recognize its shadow personality.

It is not surprising, then, that post-apartheid South Africa has lost interest for us. And why just South Africa? The rest of Africa too seems to matter little for the brave new India. The genocide in Rwanda aroused little interest in India; the same is true of the ongoing human catastrophe in Darfur. Even as an American of colour proceeds to take over the White House, showing how far colour-conscious America has succeeded in moving on, we remain oblivious of our split national mind. On the one hand, we have all kinds of programmes and laws to prevent discrimination based on gender, caste and class. On the other, we allow vulnerable rural girls to be brainwashed into believing that a fairness cream can improve their quality of life. As it is our culture poses formidable mental and social barriers to girls when they attain puberty. Some of these mental blocks make it extremely difficult for education to do what it is supposed to—namely, boost confidence in one's abilities by developing a positive self-concept. Right from early childhood, girls are socialized to perceive matrimony and motherhood as the ultimate goals of their life. A numbing array of rituals and customs are used to prepare girls for the inescapability of leaving their natal homes and for a life of dependence and silent compliance. Negative psychological attributes are compounded by everyday experience of discrimination—in all matters ranging from food intake and health care to educational opportunities. It is no surprise that the overwhelming majority of adolescent girls in India are anaemic and sickly. Seen in this larger context, the commercial enterprise to persuade them to buy a cream and use it regularly in order to look fairer acquires a poignantly inhuman character.

16

Reading is Basic to Democracy

Literacy is the foundation of school education, but in our country the term 'literacy' is used almost exclusively in the context of adults. This is not surprising, given the embarrassingly large share of India in the global count of adults who can neither read nor write. Why India's share has not dwindled significantly is partly related to the fact that the years spent by children in primary schools do not necessarily make them literate. Many who acquire a tenuous grip on literacy during those years fail to retain it in the absence of opportunities to read, compounded by elimination from school before completing the upper primary classes. Even in the case of those who acquire lasting literacy, schooling fails to impart the urge to read as a matter of habit. Those who learn to perceive reading as a means to expand knowledge and awareness are a minority. Sensational surveys of children's poor performance in reading tests throw little light on the deeper problems that the teaching of reading in India suffers from. If these problems are not addressed in an institutionalized manner, the newly enacted law on the right to education will remain ineffective.

The ability to decipher isolated letters of the alphabet is not a promising beginning of the child's progress towards becoming literate. However, this is precisely what conventional wisdom tells teachers to focus on. The wisdom is based on millennia-old practices which enabled a few children to become literate. When we apply this wisdom today, we forget that the method worked in a socio-cultural context which was altogether different from our context now. When literacy was confined to a thin upper strata of society, the teacher demanded from his wards a mastery over letters and sounds for its own sake. It took years to acquire such mastery, and the methods used to ensure it included oppressive drills and a punitive regime that can have no place today. When people feel nostalgic about traditional education, they forget that it was based on a view of childhood few would approve today, Moreover, the traditional system had no intention to cover all children. The methods it used for the teaching of reading are unsuitable for a universal system of education. The traditional approach does not recognize the child's nature and agency, nor does it respect individual differences.

The traditional methods are incompatible with modern psychology of childhood and the knowledge available today about the acquisition of language-related skills. Contemporary expertise is based on the premise that children have a natural drive to explore and understand the world; hence, reading should give them the opportunity to make sense of printed texts *from the beginning.* 'Making sense' as an experience involves relating to the text, generating a personal engagement and interpretation. If a child is not encouraged to relate to the text, or if the text they are given has little meaning or relevance, the outcome will be a crude kind of literacy which will remain isolated from the child's intellectual and emotional development. If this wider meaning of reading is applied to make an assessment, our system of primary education will arouse far greater concern than children's test scores in achievement surveys do. Persistent effort under the pressure to perform does make children capable of reading aloud a written text, but they fail to find any meaning in it. And the ability to decipher a text mechanically does not encourage children to actively look for new texts to read. The anecdote narrated by

Chinna Chacko, a former member of NCERT, in a paper she presented at the International Reading Association in 1971, continues to hold true. When she asked a child to read aloud, he asked, 'With the text or without the text?' Reflecting on the methods used in Indian schools for teaching children how to read, Chinna Chacko wrote: 'Many things are done the same way they have been done for centuries, and as a result, our primary teacher-training schools and primary schools are like museums in which old ways are carefully preserved.'

The cost of this museum-mentality is high, if we take into account the role that a reading public plays in a democratic order. The practice of democracy assumes both the habit and the capacity in all citizens to engage with matters which transcend personal or immediate reality. We can call it the metaphysics of daily life under modernity. It compels every member—without exception—to share a collective anguish and to respond to it in one way or another. Engagement with this expanded universe cannot be sustained without the tools of literacy, in addition to—and not as a substitute of—the oral means of interaction. In this model, reading serves as more than a skill; it becomes an aspect of culture. It must enable citizens to reflect on what is going on, not merely a skill to decipher printed texts. From this larger perspective, the teaching of reading during early childhood—when attitudes, habits and skills acquire life-long foundations—acquires crucial significance for the efficient functioning of democracy. This perspective implies drastic changes in the currently practiced pedagogy of reading in pre-schools and the primary classes. Instead of letter-recognition and mechanical decoding, pedagogic effort must focus on building bridges between words and meanings, and on nurturing an interpretive stance from the earliest stage. This kind of pedagogy requires meaningful texts and sustained use of children's literature. The texts used for the teaching of reading should treat the child with dignity, showing respect for the child's inner drive to interpret and relate. The sociology of the text content is equally important.

We need texts that make children excited about the social and cultural diversity that they encounter in their ethos. We also need kind and affectionate teachers who are themselves habitual readers and who can encourage each child to perceive reading as a means to pursue his or her own interest.

Over the recent decades, scholarship on reading has served as a site of ideological wars between contending schools of thought. Each time scientific study of how children learn to read makes some advance, ideological wars inevitably erupt with renewed vigour. Scholars and teacher trainers serve as both soldiers and victims of these wars. As for teachers, they just slog on, in settings which offer little opportunity or encouragement for reflection and ingenuity. Over the recent decades, teachers have heard much advice and exhortation to depart from traditional methods, but they have seldom been given sufficient and convincing rationale. The infrastructural support necessary to make new approaches successful has also been lacking. Most glaring is the absence of library support. Children's literature has remained an area of neglect and a teacher who wants her children to read a variety of books has little to choose from. A forty-part series of books published a few years ago by NCERT for beginner readers responds to this situation and makes a departure. The little books included in the *Barkha* eries, as it is called, mark several innovations, including those in design and illustration, and not just in the conception of child-centered narratives. It is the first time in India that a graded reading series, with a literary approach to reading, has been introduced. In place of the usual patronizing attitude towards children that we see in educational literature, the *Barkha* books present real children, doing the kinds of things ordinary children do at home and in the neighbourhood. A radical attempt has been made in these books not just to move away from stereotypes, but to challenge them.

Of course, a single series cannot alter the larger picture. The publishing industry involved in children's books in Hindi and most other Indian languages has a long way to go before it acquires a professional character. There has been a belief that no major progress can be expected without the state's intervention. State governments have been the main bulk purchasers of children's books, but that has not helped to improve their quality, nor has it made a difference to the business ethics of the suppliers. Many non-government organizations (NGOs) have now taken to publishing for children, and in the absence of expert guidance and institutionalized review processes, they too are churning out poor quality material, often with explicit ideological bias. State governments purchase such material with the funds that the centre provides under the Right to Education provisions. While children of the upper strata of society read imported books devoid of any resonance of the life that surrounds them, children of the lower strata find what they can in the mixed heap purchased by the government. With ideological hardening in the political sphere, children's books and magazines carrying the propaganda of religious separatism—'communalism' as it is called—are now widely distributed. After decades of criticism and advocacy, gender stereotyping is resurfacing in children's literature. It is accompanied by violent symbolism. A picture used to illustrate a story originally written by Gijubhai, the Gandhian educationist and pedagogue from Gujarat, in a book published by the National Book Trust depicts a man standing on the bent back of a woman flogging her lower back. It is hard to imagine how a state-owned publishing house, which is supposed to set standards, can let this kind of barbaric visualization pass as children's literature. But this is symptomatic of the times we live in. Competitive crudeness and suggestive violence go hand in hand with propagandist didacticism. For those who assume that universal literacy will strengthen democracy, the quality of reading material available for children must remain a major question to ponder.

A Matter of Details

17

Crafts at School

The familiar look of India's village schools presents a conundrum. How can so sad looking a space be assigned to learning, in a society which has sustained a breathtaking variety of aesthetic wealth in the objects of everyday use? When I visit the lower and upper KG classrooms of elite urban schools and find them stuffed with tacky plastic equipment, I don't know how to respond or to figure out for myself why our educational entrepreneurs, who claim to be more imaginative than government officers, are so ignorant of the resources they can draw upon from the world of India's heritage crafts to run a decent, early childhood programme. When I visit the Cottage Industries Emporium, the size of its toy section always shocks me. I then wonder how many more Kamaladevi Chattopadhyayas, Pupul Jayakars, and Laila Tyabjis, and Urmuls,[1] Self Employed Women's Associations

---

[1] Urmul Trust works with the underprivileged poor in Rajasthan to fight poverty in many ways, one of which is to help craftsmen find better markets for their goods.

(SEWAs),[2] and Sandhis[3] we will require before our icy education system melts towards the crafts.

As I see the front covers of the latest textbooks which have arrived from Rajasthan—their content being entirely another matter for despair—I am puzzled how a state with a stunning sense of colour and design can produce such barren title pages; why the Ajmer-based board office couldn't work with Tilonia to design at least the cover nicely for millions of Rajasthan's children? I should know better. There are no bridges between crafts and schools, between artisans and teachers, and between India's children and their national heritage.

The idea that handicrafts should be introduced in the school curriculum is neither new nor contentious as such, yet it looks as hard to implement now as it proved between 1937 and 1967. After it received Mahatma Gandhi's spirited advocacy, the idea moved forward despite substantial opposition which partly owed to Gandhi's politics and personality, but mainly to the historical conditions in which the independence struggle found itself during the War years. Cynicism and confusion towards new ideas, and the license to misinterpret them were as common then as they are now. Even a progressive writer and thinker like Mulk Raj Anand criticized Gandhi's proposal, ostensibly on the ground that it would legitimize and encourage child labour. The Congress–League divide became a major factor in creating a hostile ethos for a holistic craft-based basic education in the learner's mother tongue.[4]

[2] The Self Employed Women's Association (SEWA) strives to make women workers self-reliant and avail of employment security, as part of which larger movement the organization also works with crafts-persons.

[3] Sandhi is a not-for-profit organization which works to find new and innovative ways to market craft products fairly, while also working with crafts-persons to help them build their capacity and infrastructure to meet the demands of new markets.

[4] For details, see Krishna Kumar, *Prejudice and Pride*, Penguin, New Delhi, 2001; also see Joachim Oesterheld, 'National Education as a

Despite these problems, the idea did get implemented and received considerable favour after independence in several parts of India. It produced a generation which received something different from the staple of colonial schooling. If there is one word we might use to describe that something, it would be resourcefulness. The desire to make things with one's own hands and the confidence that one can make all kinds of things—indeed *anything* as one would rightly believe during childhood, if the basic urge to recreate the world is not muzzled—was what Gandhi's *nai taalim* was able to impart to quite a few among those who went to basic schools.

Despite considerable success, and due to a variety of now well-documented reasons, basic education was put to sleep in the wake of the Kothari report of 1964–6 though I am quite sure there was no explicit intention to do this. India had by then entered a new phase of its development, and in the ethos of the late 1960s, craft-centred education for children started to look like an unnecessary, idyllic whim. Several other Gandhian ideas met with a similar fate.

One major reason why the introduction of handicrafts at school looks difficult to implement now is because of the popular perception that it has failed once. The notion that ideas 'succeed' or 'fail' is entrenched in the world of decision-makers at all levels. Who wants to give a failed idea a second run when so many shining new ideas are being relentlessly supplied by the information technology (IT) industry, engineers-turned-educators, and management gurus, not to forget the multilateral agencies which invent terms and programmes quite regularly for Third World consumption? India's heritage crafts don't fit in the commonly peddled vision of 'developed'. How can they? As plastic spreads to cover our lives like a vast blanket, we cannot even remember what diversity of sensory experiences means, let alone the diversity of culture and lifestyles. The

Community Issue: The Muslim Response to the Wardha Scheme', in Krishna Kumar and Joachim Oesterheld (eds), *Education and Social Change in South Asia*, Orient Longman, New Delhi, 2007, pp. 156–95.

dream of becoming a developed nation is fast becoming like manufacturing twenty-eight flavours of ice cream with one taste.

On the other hand, handicrafts are perhaps the most representative symbol of India's cultural plurality. They signify the integration of work and values, in a context which recognizes the presence of the artist in every human being. These days we identify and honour a few exponents of crafts as 'master craftsmen'. Such a category suits and satisfies our competitive temper. Even as we discriminate between export-quality artisans from the rest, for favours like free railway passes, etc.,[5] we ought to remember that traditionally the artisan was an ordinary member of the village community. Indeed, the practice of a craft was an aspect of ordinary life, and a craft product was meant to be used in the course of everyday living.

Craft products covered all spheres of life and filled them all with the grace and a gentle light of unassuming beauty. A broom to sweep the floor, a mat or cot to sleep on, a pillow case to lay one's head down on, a pot to store water in, a doll or clay horse to play with, or a shawl to protect oneself from the cold wind—all were designed to be of use even as they infused the daily journey of life with continuous aesthetic strength, acting like a cultural drip irrigation device.

It is at this level of life's routine depth that the crafts serve as a sign of India's vast and stunning diversity. It is moderately ironical that I arrived at this understanding while walking through a museum in Pakistan. We have nothing to match it, so a few lines about it are necessary. I'm referring to Lok Virsa, located on the outskirts of Islamabad. This luminous creation of Pakistan's Department of Folklore presents the inner face of that country, a face which has sustained its radiance and

[5] For a discussion of this and other issues relevant to the crafts sector, see the introductory essay by Laila Tyabji, in *Seminar*, 523, March 2003, pp. 12–16.

diversity despite all the misfortunes that the collective national life has experienced.

Lok Virsa celebrates, in a splendour of modern museological effort and devices, the vast range of crafts practised in Pakistan. The displays communicate, in-depth, the relations between a craft, the physical geography of the region where it has flourished, its place in community life and role in shaping the local culture, its belief system and gender relations.[6] Lok Virsa explicitly celebrates women's contribution to a civilization rooted in crafts. As a South Asian visitor from India, I found Lok Virsa a moving reminder of what the crafts can do to bring us confidence, prosperity, and peace in the entire region.

It will be a good idea to try and link education and the crafts once again, but with the requisite hindsight to avoid earlier mistakes, because both sectors are facing a similar crisis. Education represents a space where a society can regenerate itself if it uses the space judiciously—the heart of education is reflection in the course of relating. It is a well-established fact that India's education system has stayed moribund partly because of the colonial legacies of administration and financial management, but mainly because of older cultural legacies which divide literacy and intellectual learning from manual work and dexterity. Our national failure to universalize elementary education and to reform the system so that it stops acting like a crude instrument of social exclusion of the so-called weaker sections, including over ten million artisans, has to do as much with the cultural character of the curriculum as with our rigid administrative practices.

Delays in implementing reforms have cost us heavily. Far from nurturing self-confidence and initiative in the young, our system makes them feel alienated from the larger society and scared of exercising personal judgement in any sphere of life. It neither trains the senses, nor does it nurture sensibility. For millions, the system continues to act, as it did in the late

[6] Ibid.

nineteenth century, as a means of getting a piece of paper which offers the promise of ever-scarce office jobs. The need to link work and education has been one of the loudest refrains in post-independence history of policy discussions, but little progress has been made in reducing the gap between mental and manual work which forms one of the oldest negative values in our culture. Gandhi's proposal for a new kind of basic education was essentially aimed at bridging that gap, but things did not go the way he had charted.

There is no reason why we cannot revisit Gandhi's idea of introducing crafts into the school curriculum, not as an extra-curricular activity, but rather as an experience which will give greater meaning and depth to the rest of the curriculum. If we think about this matter afresh and work on it with imagination and hindsight, we might reform the system of education in a manner which only the crafts can help us reform it, and in the process, we might also provide to our heritage of crafts a major institutional space where new designs, techniques, relationships, and visions can flourish. Like much else in a caste-ridden social order, both the knowledge and skill aspects of crafts have suffered from the effects of isolation and stagnation. Linking formal education with crafts could help foster creativity in both.

Before I proceed to discuss this proposed linkage further, I would like to briefly examine the crisis which the crafts are facing in the economic world, with the help of two books, *The Making of a Cybertariat* by Ursula Huws[7] and *The Real World of Technology* by Ursula Franklin.[8]

Ursula Huws is a labour economist whose commitment to feminism and Marxism disqualifies her from being called a Luddite. Her argument in the only book she has published in a long career of fighting for workers' rights in England is that something special is happening in the history of technology and

[7] Monthly Review Press, New York, 2005.
[8] Anansi, Toronto, 1990; revised in 1999.

social relations, and that we are passing through a watershed which demands a new level of human ingenuity to fight ideological fatigue. An equilibrium reached in employer–worker relations after the Second World War is caving in, she argues. Many such break-points have occurred in the history of technology, each one representing a new level of capital being invested to incorporate human skills in technology itself and make the owners of skills redundant—but the current one is more pervasive. Huws shows us that the direction science and technology take depends on where profits and hence investments take us; in other words, the growth of technology and the science that supports it has to do with values and intentions.

Huws gives numerous examples, one being that of the emerging 'cybertariat' which has incorporated all the skills that office-workers—mostly women in the Western world—had used to develop a collective self-identity over the post-war decades. It matters no more how well you can design a letter and format it, or how dexterously you can correct the errors made in the first draft. The craft element in the secretary's job has been withdrawn. The desktop has centuries of craftsmanship incorporated in it; the user now merely clicks at the required sign, one of the several offered in the menu, 'format', 'view', or simply 'help'. Huws brings out the change this will cause in economic and cultural relations, especially in the sphere of secular, work-based identity. In the process of giving us several such examples, she gives us a clue to how to define crafts—as something which requires care, personal attention, and develops an identity by conveying: 'This is what I do well; this is who I am.'

The crisis faced by crafts is really a reflection of a larger dis-equilibrium which identity conflicts represent sharply enough for social scientists, even economists, to take notice of. Take, for example, tailoring. What makes it a craft is the relationship shared with a person which shapes the concern and care shown in the cutting, stitching, and the final, finer work. When the individual a tailor is stitching for, turns into a body size, the craft might as well vanish into a software which leaves the garment factory worker with no judgement to exercise, only the relevant buttons to press at desired moments.

Those of us who are making a case for heritage crafts in the school curriculum are obviously greatly disturbed by the economic, and technological changes we notice around us. Such changes have occurred earlier in the history of crafts as well, but this time the crisis is likely to spread faster. There are countries which have managed to protect their crafts by reconciling to the new reality and working within it. South Africa is one such country where organization and marketing of craft products are now tightly linked to commerce and tourism. In India too, this effort is under way, though the scale of our operation is quite limited and our progress slow. With good management minds applied in due course, I am sure we will succeed in creating a large enough market for our crafts, and perhaps a considerable number of craftsmen and craftswomen will find it possible to make a living, at least a better living than they are able to afford at present.

Finding a larger clientele for craft products is indeed a major challenge by itself, but the future of crafts will be shaped by many more decisions and initiatives. Perhaps the most important ones will be about the social status of artisans in India's democracy. Education is undoubtedly a major factor which will shape the future of artisans and the crafts they practise. Not just education of their children, but also the links that education, as a system, might allow to be formed between the knowledge and skill embedded in India's craft heritage, will determine how capable our crafts become in surviving the onslaught of the neo-liberal doctrine, and after ensuring survival, in shaping the future of our civilization. The present moment offers little room for complacency.

In her book, *The Real World of Technology*, Ursula Franklin makes a distinction between holistic and prescriptive technologies. The basis of this distinction is whether the technology permits individuals to control it. Whereas prescriptive technologies are efficient and allow large numbers of people to act as a group, they transfer control over all aspects of the work to someone above. Moreover, each person knows only how to do the bit for which he or she is responsible. In holistic technology, people control the process of their own work from beginning to end. Decisions are taken while a product is being worked on by the artisan, not by someone with higher authority.

Franklin, who is among Canada's foremost experimental physicists, gives the example of casting of large vessels in ancient China to illustrate the earliest example of prescriptive technology. Work was organized in a series of separately implemented tasks in which a large number of people were involved, all complying with the precise specifications supervised by a boss or manager. She illustrates holistic technology with the help of handicrafts which require the individual creator of an object to conceptualize it, work on it, and complete it. The two kinds of technologies, Franklin says, 'involve distinctly different specializations and divisions of labour, and consequently they have very different social and political implications'.[9]

Prescriptive technology promotes a culture of compliance; this happened in ancient China, Franklin argues, by shaping social and political thought and giving rise to the earliest known example of a bureaucracy. Holistic technology, used in a vast variety of crafts, shaped social and political institutions in Europe. During the industrial revolution, prescriptive technologies 'spread like an oil slick', Franklin says, but she argues that the element of choice continues to be relevant. Although the survival of holistic technologies has become more precarious, there are urgent reasons (such as the scarcity of environmental resources and the political crisis of different kinds which both the highly industrialized and the

[9] Ursula Franklin, *The Real World of Technology*, p. 10.

less industrialized countries are facing) to exercise discretion and choice to identify the spheres in which the two kinds of technologies need to be deployed.

For countries which have a long tradition of handicrafts, the process of modernizing industries has meant considerable anguish and a sense of threat for social groups who specialize in a certain handicraft and depend on it for their survival. This kind of anguish has been expressed in India quite continuously by patrons of handicrafts, many of whom have struggled hard for their entire careers to secure a place for the crafts in the state's plans for economic development. While this battle must continue, a space for the survival and advancement of crafts needs to be claimed within the system of school education. This is what the NCF, 2005, seeks to do.

The Focus Group report for heritage crafts prepared under the NCF exercise points out that crafts have, over the centuries, served as a resource for both metaphors and ideas in Indian philosophy, metaphysics, art, and social living. The report says, 'craft—both in theory and in practice—can be a powerful tool of emotional, economic, and intellectual empowerment for children at all levels, locations, and sectors of school and society.'[10] This claim should suffice to inspire any school principal or state education officer to give crafts a chance.

The introduction of crafts in the school curriculum has the potential to trigger several long-desired reforms in the system of education. To realize the full potential of a crafts curriculum, a number of preparatory steps would have to be taken. One has to do with how we organize the availability of equipment and material necessary for the teaching of crafts in schools which opt for it. If we treat this task as a question of purchase and supply, we might end up repeating the mistakes made in the course of Operation Blackboard in the late 1980s. There

[10] National Focus Group, Position Paper on *Heritage Crafts*, National Council of Educational Research and Training (NCERT), New Delhi, 2006.

are alternatives.

For private (or 'public' as they are known in India) schools, there is perhaps no problem in making their own decisions about where to acquire the equipment they want, such as looms, cloth, colours, and threads, wood, clay or kilns from. In private schools, the real challenge lies in changing the management's—and often the principal's—mind about tinsel, gloss, and air-conditioning pointing to the way forward. The lifestyle and demands of the urban elite parent is what private schools will have to contend with when they attempt to find a space for the crafts in their stuffed timetables. The fear that their boys will miss the IIT entrance if they spend time learning how to make a shoe, after reading Galsworthy's 'Quality'[11] in their English textbook, will deter a lot of principals and heads of management committees.

A far bigger systemic challenge faces the government school system, including its more privileged sub-systems represented by Kendriya and Navodaya Vidyalayas. Government schools are not treated like individual institutions. Everything happens because of a directive from above, and it applies to all schools. Many great ideas of reform have failed to make a dent because of the failure to treat each government school as an autonomous unit whose principal and teachers should have the professional freedom to make decisions on certain matters within a framework of choices.

If crafts are introduced as a decision taken by an enlightened state director, that will guarantee its demise even as it attempts to begin. Unsuitable choices will be made, equipment and material will be supplied through procedures prone to corruption, and in the end, this material will remain locked in boxes. Instead, if only an outline is proposed and individual

---

[11] This short story narrates how the industrial revolution affected the life and cultural values of village society in England. The story revolves around a shoemaker whose judgement and skill are unmatched by mass-produced footwear.

schools are allowed to choose the craft they want to introduce, and the sources where they will acquire the relevant equipment and material, the principal can be legitimately expected to feel responsible for the outcome of the project. This is what the NCF has suggested as a general reform with wide-ranging implications.[12] Crafts are a good starting point to moot the idea of institutional autonomy.

Schools which introduce crafts in their curriculum should involve locally available crafts-persons to work with children and teachers. There is hardly a region in India which does not have its own craft traditions and people who still practise these despite the stress they are under. As the National Focus Group on Heritage Crafts passionately pleads, these locally available crafts-persons must be paid a decent honorarium when they are invited to work with school teachers and children. Linking craft teaching with the traditional school subjects, instead of treating them as an extra-curricular add-on, is necessary to firmly entrench work-related values and ethics in the school's life.[13]

Schools which decide to initiate craft teaching should draw connections between different aspects of the chosen craft and the other subjects. For instance, mathematics can be linked with material and design aspects, whereas science can be taught while studying the processes involved in crafts like pottery. The vocabulary specific to a craft can be utilized and ramified in language and literature classes with the help of relevant literary material (such as Phanishwarnath Renu's short story, 'Thes'[14] or Galsworthy's story 'Quality' which has been referred

[12] The National Focus Group on Heritage Crafts (see note 10) lists a number of sources from which advice can be sought regarding crafts and where to obtain the required materials and information.

[13] For details, see National Focus Group, Position Paper on *Work and Education*, National Council of Educational Research and Training (NCERT), New Delhi, 2007.

[14] Phanishwarnath Renu's short story.

to earlier). The social geography of a craft (that is, who are its practitioners, where are their products sent and sold for use, etc.) can be linked to the social science curriculum.

Teaching crafts at school must also be seen as an aspect of art education. The existing art curriculum tends to focus on the classical traditions and ignores the folk traditions in which the crafts are usually embedded. There is an urgent need to redefine the art curriculum in all major areas, that is, music, dance, theatre, and the visual arts, to incorporate folk traditions and styles. In the context of such a redefinition, craft programmes can be accommodated within a broader art education framework. This is not a plea for ignoring the other possibilities that a crafts programme can open up, such as linkages with vocational training which leads towards manufacturing skills and attitudes. These also lie within the domain of craft education but they need not form the main terrain or basis of craft advocacy, partly because we have experienced this line in the Gandhian phase without much success, and also because we have no immediate reason to expect a sudden alleviation of the crisis which the crafts are facing in the context of economic survival.

Schools which opt for a crafts-in-curriculum project can shed their worries about value education. The term 'value education' is a reminder of the extent to which our expectations from education per se have declined. One comes across different kinds of programmes aimed at putting values into education, as if what has been going on in schools can now be infused with a handful of values. Crafts will play this role in a manner which many may not easily recognize because the value component of craft-learning is subtle.

When children learn a craft, they participate in a process which gives the individual learner ample room to experiment within a warm but demanding tradition of rigour. Standards of correctness rise from one's own work. The ability to redo or correct oneself is nurtured spontaneously, provided that the teacher is not oppressive and that the principal is not planning to display children's 'best' products at the annual day function to be admired by a VIP chief guest. Higher-order ethical values arise in the context of relations with others, including relations with nature. The late David Horsburgh explained how the material one works on teaches us how to relate to it: 'If we ill-treat a piece of wood we are trying to carve, it breaks.'

Marjorie Sykes, in her book on life with Gandhi,[15] recounts her conversations with children and teachers who had learnt spinning as part of the basic education programme. The teachers told her that they pick cotton bolls only when they are fully ripe, for then 'a gentle touch is all that is needed, they come away easily. If they don't, they are not yet ready for picking. We should wait another few days. We should not be impatient or greedy.' Sykes comment is: 'That was education too, education in how to handle other living things, plants and animals, with respect for the natural cycle of their own lives—education in one aspect of non-violence'.[16]

Many other aspects of craft learning will emerge as being relevant to education in ethics when schools and teacher training institutions start working with artisans. A different sense of time and rigour, personal care for the product, and a sense of detail are normal features of any craft experience. Whether you embroider a handkerchief or carve a piece of wood, you enter into a rhythm of self-discovery, joy, and comfort. If you practise a craft in an ethos which guarantees individual dignity and fairness, you gain self-confidence of a kind nothing else can give.

[15] Jehangir P. Patel and Marjorie Sykes, *Gandhi: His Gift of the Fight*, Friends Rural Centre, Rasulia, 1987.

[16] Ibid., p. 54.

18

The Woman with a Broom

Looking at the woman assembling dry leaves and plasticized wrappers with her long, municipal broom outside my door, I sit down to practise Zen master Thich Nhat Hanh's search for 'interbeing' in the hope that it will reveal a secret of education my university does not know.

Every morning she comes, knocking out another little bit of the earth's soil cover with her broom which is designed to do this. The design comes from long tradition, from times when no one had a reason to worry about God's gifts like the earth's surface. Today we have plenty of reason to worry, for our city is already so full of dust—the carrier of discomfort and illness, a ubiquitous symbol of the degradation of the soil. We should have designed brooms that don't break the earth's surface, but we haven't. Every morning a few million hard brooms create little eddies of dust as they break the already broken bits of soil further. We have not designed better brooms for reasons I can imagine; reasons like the low status of the woman who uses the broom as an instrument of livelihood. Her life, comfort, and efficiency do not matter enough to deserve the attention of professional designers.

Maybe, someone has designed a better, surface-friendly broom, and the new design has not reached the woman sweeping outside my house for the same reason for which the late David Horsburgh's textbooks, though better than the

NCERT's, have not reached the school whose children would soon walk by my house. They are children of *karmacharis*—'class four' employees of my university. Most of these children fail in the high school examination or pass with poor marks. The curriculum proves too difficult for them to negotiate, solely dependent as they are on badly written and even more badly produced state textbooks, translated in a strange and cruel Hindi from the English original. The examination makes no distinction between these children and those studying in private schools where English is used as a medium of instruction and children buy a whole range of extra material to supplement the prescribed textbooks. The teachers of these private schools have a stronger motivation to be more attentive. Many of the students take expensive coaching to gain a few percentage points for entry into the prestigious Indian Institutes of Technology (IITs).

As a premiere institution of technology research, the IIT could well have been the place where someone might design a surface-friendly broom. If the woman sweeping in front of my door has a child, and if the child is a boy, he has, in principle, a chance equal to anyone else's of going to the IIT when he grows up. It is to maintain this parity of chance that the system of education compels every school to follow the same syllabus and take the same examination. Between the two public examinations taken at the end of grades ten and twelve, some 80 per cent of the country's children who had survived in the system up to grade ten—already less than a third of the total who had started attending school ten years earlier—are eliminated. These are mostly children studying in government schools in both urban and rural areas; they are children of the 'weaker', though politically stronger, sections of society.

She gathers the dry leaves of jamun, ashoka, and neem into a pile, and gingerly touches the pile with a burning matchstick before leaving the site for the day. This habit of hers annoys me no end.

The sight of little burning piles of leaves is common in our city and in the university campus. My own institute, which trains teachers for schools, has no other method of disposing of dry leaves and other garbage. I have discussed this matter with the gardeners and the sweepers of my institute, explaining to them the dangers of global warming to which the burning of garbage makes a contribution as well as the more immediate risk of further pollution in Delhi. They always agree with my criticism and concern; so do the gardeners in the university campus, but the practice does not stop. One of the gardeners told me in the course of one of our dialogues that it would be cumbersome and difficult to make a sufficient number of pits if all the leaves in the campus were to be buried rather than burnt. Apart from space for that many pits, the labour required to dig would be difficult to muster. I doubt if anyone has actually calculated the space and the labour needed for leaf-pits in the campus, let alone the city. It seems that the point about advocating leaf-burial for compost, as an alternative to leaf-piles for burning, is one of those suggestions that are right and proper, even scientific, but no one has worked it out in detail for trial.

The gardener told me that if the university really wanted the leaves falling off the enormous number of deciduous trees in the campus to be buried, it would have to hire or buy extra space to make a sufficient number of pits. Extra seasonal labour would have to be hired too. More plausible, he thought, would be to get used to seeing dry leaves around in the season when they fall. Beautiful though they look, I thought, accepting them lying around would require a considerable change of attitude— from one of regarding dry leaves as garbage to one of looking at them with pleasure and compassion. The woman who must sweep and burn them as a matter of duty would likely be happy too if the change of attitude took place among the people she serves. For now, we must find a way to calm our anguish over her routine act of burning the little piles she makes. Preferring burial to burning is like so many other things written in our textbooks—good to memorize, but much too vague for real life. No wonder they are ignored; even major things that should not be ignored are not given thought because they are presented so vaguely. Take, for instance, the instruction that rainwater must not be allowed to stand in drains or pits. What good does this excellent idea do to anyone, I have often wondered. What it might mean for a child or a group of children, hopefully with their teacher, to allow the stagnant water in a blocked drain to flow has not been worked out in any detail by our textbook writers, or else they would have acknowledged the difficulties involved in the task. The simple mention they make of it, without an accompanying acknowledgement of the difficulties involved in it, indicates that they don't expect it to be taken seriously. No wonder our country is full of blocked drains and roadside pools of standing water.

Why textbooks alone, the national policy on education is also full of such ideas—correct and worthy of everyone's support, but much too general or vague to be followed up in action. I know from my personal experience of attending policy meetings how typical it is of senior civil servants like a secretary or joint secretary to say that we, the members, need only to decide the broad principles or plan, and that we need not worry about 'matters of detail'. A distinct odium is attached to those words—'matters of detail'. Lower level officials and clerks are supposed to look after them. It happens all the time. Major schemes failed to make a difference because matters of detail were not worked out by the same people who proposed the schemes. Despite repeated failure, we don't learn the point that matters of detail are the heart of educational reform, or for that matter, reform in any sphere. I recall a meeting I attended in the mid-1980s. It had been called to determine what supplies were to be made to rural primary schools under 'Operation Blackboard'. I suggested a globe to be included in the list. Some people wondered why a primary school needed a globe when the syllabus emphasized local and regional geography. After some discussion on the importance of nurturing children's natural curiosity, etc., the item 'globe' was entered in the list of supplies to be made. I wanted to ensure that the entry would specify 'wooden globe', for I was afraid that the finance committee would instinctively opt for the cheaper, plastic globe. I was told that this was a matter of detail, so it would be looked after at the relevant level. Years later when I visited a village primary school where the supplies of Operation Blackboard material had been made, I asked the headmaster how the globe was being used. He was reluctant to talk about it, even to show it. Finally when he brought it out, I saw that it was a plastic globe, torn and flattened, which was a natural thing to have happened to a plastic globe in a school for little children. A matter of detail had prevailed in the end.

Apart from dry leaves of roadside trees, the little burning pile in front of my house contains bits and pieces of garbage, consisting of paper, plastic, and plasticized paper. More specifically, the garbage contains potato chip bags, ice-cream wrappers, 'pan parag' pouches, plastic carry bags or 'pinnis', peanut and corn peels, and pieces of greasy paper used for holding a samosa or bhatoora. All of these items are residues of the snacks that students, standing beside the vendors, eat during the day. Pieces of paper are also dropped by students who pass by on their way to one of the campus colleges or back home. During the student union election every year, little cards carrying the name of a candidate or pamphlets naming a slate of candidates are handed out in thousands. The morning after the election these cards and pamphlets cover large patches of road all over the campus, waiting for sweepers to gather and burn them. It would be nice to imagine the elected student union being asked to pay for the extra work that the sweepers have to do; even nicer would be to imagine the newly elected members sweeping the roads themselves. I can well imagine one of them answering back, reminding us that the members of the Uttar Pradesh legislative assembly were never asked to pay for refurnishing the assembly house after it had been ransacked by the members themselves when they were hitting each other with whatever they could lay their hands on, including microphones. A retributive measure taken with an eye on teaching a lesson seems to have no place in our civic life.

Under the prevailing circumstances, it cannot be imagined that my university can persuade or instruct the students not to throw garbage around. Throwing bits and pieces of things around is treated as a special kind of right. At the beautiful flower show we have every spring, the *shamyana* gate gets littered with torn entry tickets soon after the opening ceremony. Perhaps some of the students who eat snacks on the roadside do want to throw garbage into a bin, but where are the bins? The city of Delhi has rather few garbage bins; they are so few I can visualize them. Yet, all children are taught in schools, starting with grade four, that garbage must be thrown into a bin. I have sat in at least fifty lessons where this topic was being taught in the late elementary classes. I cannot remember a single occasion when a child said, 'M'am, there are no garbage bins in our locality, so how can we use them?' Apparently, children learn early in their school career that what they learn from their teachers and textbooks need not have a relation with reality or behaviour. The students who attend my university do, of course, know well that it is a good idea to keep roads and sidewalks clean, that garbage disposal is a big problem in modern living, that filth is linked to serious diseases. They study all this before coming to college. These things are so elementary that they cannot figure in the university syllabus. Not even the BEd syllabus of my institute includes such things, for it is assumed that our trainees know them well, and indeed they do. When I ask them in my tutorial class why there is so much dirt on the street, or why our own institute is so unkempt, they inevitably say, 'The sweepers don't work properly.' Some always add that the sweepers have become lazy and smug because of the reservation policy.

To end with a summary of sorts, I have written this short account of a train of thought out of love for my profession, not out of a desire to hurt anyone, least of all those who have tried to improve education in their official capacities or independently. The list of people who have tried to change Indian education in this century starts with Tagore and Gandhi. I feel we have not paid enough attention to the details required to put their ideas into practice; in fact, we discarded them much too early. We must ponder on these and other failures deeply to identify better ways to use new ideas in future. Objectives and principles are important, but they are somewhat meaningless if they are not accompanied by smaller thoughts, about things that occur to you when you start working with a group of children or even a single child. Details strike you if you look intently at a problem, keeping in mind the context in which the problem must be faced. What must happen in a classroom full of children from morning to afternoon is a question of the highest order for national reconstruction. If we approach this question without focusing our attention on the faces of the children, the state of the classroom, the personality and preparedness of the teacher, and the quality of the textbooks and other material available to the teacher, then we are likely to do no better in the near future than we are doing at present. Small details, if ignored, tend to destroy big plans.

19

Watching as Work

Now that a court order has made dissection of animals optional for biology students, I wonder if another court order can be sought to make observation of nature a requirement for science study. As things stand, a student can get through school and college with shining success without developing the ability to notice details in natural phenomena. There are children whose entire knowledge of nature comes from books, the blackboard, and a few laboratory experiments. In the case of some, we can add a computer monitor. Since the science syllabi are already so packed with facts, I wish the English syllabi might include a reading of the late Konrad Lorenz's *King Solomon's Ring*,[1] a delightful classic on animal behaviour. Perhaps a similar purpose would be served by *Jungle and Backyard*,[2] a collection of essays by the late M. Krishnan. It is a pity our children get no taste of the pleasure that careful observation of a cat, a fish, or a tree in natural circumstances can bring.

A few years ago when Ahmedabad's Centre for Environmental Education brought out a tiny manual on watching a tree, I thought it would make a difference. But alas, books which

[1] Meridian, USA, [1952] 1997.
[2] Oxford University Press, New Delhi, 1995.

are not fortunate enough to gain the status of textbooks mean
nothing in our system. Otherwise, a remarkable book on trees
written by Chakravarti S. Venkatesh and published by the
NCERT some twenty years ago would have made an impact.
The kind of leisure it demands, and the freedom to connect
things in one's mind, it assumes, have no place in our schools
because they are fixated on textbooks and a textbook-based
examination. This book has not sold well mainly because it is not
a textbook.

Things are not radically different in most parts of the world,
but some systems do manage to put in opportunities for relaxed
observation here and there. I recall meeting a large group of
children outside the wolf's compound in the Tokyo zoo. Several
hours later, when I had completed my tour of the zoo and was
on my way out, I noticed the children and their teacher still
busy with the wolf. They had spent the day watching every part
and behaviour of the wolf, taking notes and comparing their
observations with those given in the books they were carrying.

Our children, of course, never get this kind of opportunity
or training. A visit to the zoo means seeing everything, just
as our syllabi provide a cursory, whirlwind coverage of every
topic and fact. I have a lingering, painful memory which is
relevant here, though it is not about nature study. A group
of schoolboys was rushing past the photo exhibition at the
Sabarmati Ashram in Ahmedabad, and their teachers were
busy making sure that no one was left behind. Despite the
teachers' vigilance, two boys managed to stop at a picture for
a few minutes, noticing something unusual in it. As I watched
in horror, one of the teachers came back looking for the boys
and the first thing she did on finding them was to slap and scold
them for staying behind.

Anyone who has hung around school corridors would know
that teachers give priority to maintaining group discipline over
appreciating individual curiosity or effort. But it is hardly fair to
blame teachers for this instinct. They decipher their role in the
institutional ethos and in the social milieu as a whole. A culture

featuring lack of appreciation, or rather contempt, for initiative and imagination pervades the system, and teachers simply grow into it. The best of them find it hard to resist conforming to the existing pattern, especially to the pressure to cover the syllabus superficially. One of the best teachers trained by my institute told me when I met her in a school that she was now studying law. Finding me a little astonished she said, 'It's impossible to change anything in the system as a teacher. Maybe I'll have a chance to press for change as a lawyer.'

The case against dissection proves her point. There was no good reason why this case should have gone to a court in the first place. Apparently the system of education has become incapable of reforming itself. The only pressure that matters is judicial. I now hear that an organization called Parents Forum has gone to court in order to seek the examinee's right to see his or her answer book after evaluation and to apply for re-evaluation. There is no reason why these rights cannot be granted without judicial intervention. The system of examination will gain much needed transparency and public confidence if these facilities are incorporated into present-day routines.

There is a common belief that progressive measures first enter the system through schools looking after the wealthier sections of society. This did happen in certain countries, but the history of education in many others suggests that innovations have occurred more often in response to the needs of the weaker and vulnerable sections of society. How our system will eventually respond to the demands for change is not yet clear. For a while it seemed that schools where richer kids go might set the pattern for changes like leisurely, out-of-school work in science and social science subjects. Recent trends suggest that these schools are more worried about isolating their children from the natural and the social environments than about introducing significant changes in the curriculum. Adding expensive frills to the building or staging a spectacular annual function gains priority over buying multiple copies of useful books for the library. Central air-conditioning is advertised as an attraction, and one school has gone as far as providing air-conditioned buses with a little fan above every seat.

One can hardly imagine that schools of this kind will permit children to spend a day observing a stagnant pond. This would be regarded as a big waste of time. Teachers of our elite schools don't mind children submitting project work copied from computerized encyclopaedias for it saves time, they say. As one might expect, the ethos of hurried, perfunctory completion of work which characterizes the elite schools is serving as a model for state-run schools. Functioning with skimpy facilities, state schools compete as best as they can with private schools, typically by promoting cramming and other regressive practices which promise high marks in the non-discerning examination system. The size of prescribed syllabi and the dull character of textbooks generally rules out what room there may be in an individual teacher's style for personal enquiry and observation.

There is, of course, nothing new about this kind of critique; the Secondary Education Commission had said as much in the early 1950s in the vocabulary current at that time. The question why change has eluded the system tends to invite a host of theories, but the one thing we cannot overlook is that the concept of knowledge underpinning the system has a lot to do with the resilience our schools have shown. The idea that a great deal of children's knowledge comes from their day-to-day experience is just not appreciated in our schools and society. The obsolete belief that children simply absorb the information the teacher gives them, that children learn mainly by imitation, is still far too deeply entrenched. No wonder our schools place so much stress on children learning the right answers, mainly the names of objects, processes, and events. Richard P. Feynman[3] has recalled the story of how, when he was a little boy, he asked his father to name a certain bird. His father told

[3] *Surely You're Joking, Mr. Feynman: Adventures of a Curious Character*, W.W. Norton, New York, 1977.

him what the bird was called in different languages. But these names don't matter, the father said; what is really important is to observe the bird carefully. Perhaps a lot of teachers and parents can understand this story but they lack the will to reshape their daily practice in line with Feynman's father.

20

Lotus Syndrome

Speaking at a Sainik School on its annual function, Jammu and Kashmir chief minister, Mufti Mohammed Sayeed, made the oft-repeated plea that talented students from the weaker sections of society should be given special treatment. This kind of concern for the more capable among the poor carries some obvious assumptions. One is that children of the poor can be divided into two sharp categories—the talented and the ordinary—and that such a classification can be made on reliable grounds. A more problematic assumption is that children who fall in the first category matter more.

Once we accept this way of looking at children from lower-income strata, the state's responsibility to ensure social justice takes on a simple character. Instead of ensuring that every child gets a real educational opportunity, the state feels free to focus its attention on the few who qualify to be called talented. This is what the fifteen-year-old Navodaya Scheme is all about, and now we have similar schemes in many states which allow the supposedly more intelligent among the poor to be segregated from the rest for special treatment.

During his speech, Mr Sayeed made the revelation that ten talented children from among the needy had been selected for admission, at the government's expense, to the Delhi Public School's (DPS) branch in the state. The chief minister's speech indicates that he doesn't hold state schools in high regard.

Mr Sayeed's view is that the talented deserve to be identified and set apart from the ones who apparently do not possess recognizable talent. Such a perception is quite common and has a long history in our culture. It finds expression in several popular symbols and metaphors, one of which is that of the lotus. Since ancient times, the man of knowledge is regarded as the lotus flower which stays above the muddy water in which it grows. This symbolism sat well with a hierarchical social order which justified acute forms of segregation, but it does not sit well with the vision of a society in which everyone matters and an equal educational opportunity is supposed to exist for all.

The modern egalitarian dream has a special relevance to the industrial process of production which brings about division of labour and demands excellence from everybody. There are no roles one might call insignificant in an industrial order. The man who was watching the pressure of gas on the tragic night in Bhopal was probably not so highly placed in the hierarchy. If that is the reason why those who mattered more didn't hear his repeated warning that the pressure was getting too high, then the story has a deeper grimness than the measly compensation given to the victims evokes.

Similar thoughts come to mind when one sees the men sent to fix open manholes. Their lack of status is reflected in the tools they carry and the indifference they show to replacing the manhole cover flush with the road as it should be. The social cost of their lack of status and the fact that they are supposed to derive no great satisfaction from their work is incurred on the day someone trips on the ill-fitted cover. India is blessed with a great number of people who might show excellence in top jobs in their respective establishments, but those available to do middle or lower rung jobs are hardly ever expected to show excellence in their performance. Indeed, we do not use the word 'excellence' for such jobs. Our reluctance is rooted in the caste system which denies dignity of labour. This attitude seems to have been reinforced by monarchical rule in certain regions. These tenacious legacies can't be expected to surrender to the regime of democracy without friction. In fact, the success of democracy has triggered a backlash, one reaction being a hankering after hierarchy.

A popular weekly devoted a whole special issue a few years ago to the fifty Indians who matter, suggesting that others didn't. I once heard a high-ranking official of the CBSE say that its results were quite accurate in identifying the top 15 per cent of children who matter for India's progress. A similar perception runs through state schemes which offer special or privileged budgetary treatment to a few even as the vast majority of children are left to do whatever they can in schools where the basic necessities of education are inadequate or shoddy. Each time the state adopts a scheme to give an educational privilege to a few students, it acknowledges that it cannot reform the system as a whole. Typically, the state first creates a two-tier system, then draws up a populist scheme to improve the second tier, and this process goes on. The parallel sub-system of private schools has been allowed and encouraged to grow wild, to the extent that some of them now flaunt air-conditioned classrooms and buses, food ordered from five-star hotels, and annual functions outsourced to event managers.

So long as political leaders, and not just ordinary people, continue to believe that a few talented individuals can make a difference, India's progress towards becoming a modern society will remain slow and bumpy, even if the rate of economic growth remains high; a sense of fairness, conveyed by a modicum of equal opportunity, is a necessary condition for modernization. If these painkillers are withdrawn in the name of nurturing talent in islands of excellence we will end up jeopardizing the entire project. Vivekananda had asked for 100,000 dedicated men and women to transform India. Today, this won't suffice. Indeed, nothing less than universal education of a certain basic quality— which gives all children a comparable chance to develop, will do.

It is true that equality takes long to become real, and it may look as if in the short run a concern for equality harms quality. Such a perception guided planners of education to opt for islands of excellence. The IITs and the Indian Institutes of Management (IIMs) are examples of this approach in higher education while Navodaya Vidyalayas illustrate it at the school level. The perspective these institutions represent might have had some justification when economic growth was slow and the pressure of the articulate, higher income status was high. Today, India should make more sensible choices, partly because it can afford to do so, but mainly because the masses too have become somewhat articulate. Pedagogic modernization demands that we recognize the richness of experience associated with diversity of social backgrounds in the classroom. What is learnt is just as important as the ethos in which it is learnt. Homogeneity in the classroom implies a limited pool of the common resources of learning, such as language, culture, and personality.

21

Metaphors of Innovation

The question of innovations and their relation to reform has always intrigued me. Two metaphors that might help us to focus on this issue are: one, a sapling that requires a tree guard around it to grow safely to a point when the tree guard can be taken off and a seed planted in a rock, either by chance or by design. It cannot move, and must grow there. Similarities between these metaphors are obvious, and probably equally obvious are the very critical differences. The fact that an innovation is usually an isolated event is obvious in both those metaphors. Innovative activity is somewhat isolated from the rest of the system. The sapling and the seed both convey a sense of isolation. There is also the question of survival. In both situations, survival is a struggle. In the history of education across the world, you will not find an example of an innovation that was a comfortable exercise, welcome from the very beginning. For an innovative attempt in education to survive for any length of time is almost a miracle. There is also a third similarity: both metaphors suggest an eventual change in the landscape. If the sapling does grow up to a point where it becomes a tree of a certain height, of certain strength, then it will change the landscape or the street. Were the seed to grow through the rock, it would change the landscape. India is a land where peepul trees typically grow within rocks; you can see them growing over rocks, completely changing the appearance of the rock, the peepul's roots growing through the cracks. With time, the rock will begin to crack; it crumbles, and the landscape changes. This eventual promise of a change in the landscape is inbuilt in both these metaphors.

In an experiment like Shanti Niketan, one of the greatest experiments in education in twentieth-century India, both these aspects can be seen. Tagore protected the experiment with his own money and effort, taking it away from the big city and making sure that nothing was done in it that would make it a part of the system, which he regarded as evil. At the same time, he knew that the landscape was rocky, and for Shanti Niketan to grow, constant battles against hostile and uncomprehending authorities and critics would have to be fought. For this reason, a certain depression had set in, in the poet's mind, fairly early. By the time he was dying, he was aware that the principles of Shanti Niketan would be difficult to protect.

Now let us look at the crucial differences between these two metaphors. The pre-suppositions are different. In the sapling metaphor, we can see that there is a consensus about the need to protect it. People understand why it needs to be protected, and so the tree guard is installed. In the second metaphor of the seed in a rock, there is an inherent opposition: despite the rock, the seed will grow and the landscape will change. The change is radical, and destructive to the rock. The sapling metaphor presupposes stability in intentions: the need is to protect a weak tree as it grows, and the protection will continue to be extended to it for as long as it is needed. There needs to be a consensus among the various parties involved about why the sapling needs to be protected, and from whom. We don't want a situation where suddenly the consensus changes: instead of the sapling, people may argue that the cows need protection, and should be allowed free access to saplings. I am not implying any political satire here: just that there is need for stability in consensus, stability of a political kind, in the widest sense of the term. In the second case, of the rock being cracked open by the seed when it grows, one is aware of the oppositional design for which one seed is hardly sufficient. Many seeds are required, growing in the crevices of the rock at different locations. Also, for the landscape to change eventually, the seed has to be of a fairly strong variety like the peepul. Perhaps several failed attempts will first have to be made before a sapling grows through the rock.

Now for some more direct, less metaphorical analysis: it bears repetition that, by nature, innovations are political processes; they involve political initiative. Every innovation challenges the existing state of power relations, and these power relations are of a kind that cannot be overcome merely by change of vocabulary. For instance, when we talk about empowering teachers, we trivialize the concept of power as it prevails in politics. We know that most teachers are even meeker today than they were two decades ago. We cannot talk about the teacher being empowered unless those placed above the teacher lose some of their power. Empowerment is not just about learning a few skills or techniques. The system hardly offers the teacher dignity and autonomy in fulfilling his or her responsibility. We cannot talk of innovations in the system without a full awareness that innovations will also upset power relations that already exist, within which teachers have little power.

If innovations are to be part of the mainstream, and not merely isolated experiments, it is important to build political consensus. It is necessary that the ethos be appreciative of the need for innovation, and not perceive these as threatening. These innovations will, ultimately, be enriching to politics itself. If this idea does not extend fully to those horizons, it is likely that innovations will be seen as temporary. The system may simply wait around for the innovation to die out, closing off the space for change and growth. We know from our study of climate that a low-pressure zone is usually a fleeting zone. High-pressure areas generate strong winds, and the winds coming from the high-pressure zones will fill up the space, blowing into the low-pressure areas. That is more or less what happens to innovations of either kind—either the sapling or the seed-in-the-rock kind. They create a low-pressure zone in the political landscape, and strong winds from the high-pressure zones begin to blow towards this low-pressure area in a determined attempt to recover that space. This political process intensifies as innovations mature, as they begin to succeed, and at this point it becomes very critical whether the perception of the innovation is also changing or not. Is the innovation seen as a temporary experimental measure, sustained through the personal interest and participation of some officials, or has it been embedded in the system, seen as necessary? It is necessary to understand the perceptions of stakeholders, as these will determine whether the innovations will be stages in a system's transition. So the process of innovation has a kind of meta-requirement of building an ethos in which there is greater receptivity. Indeed, if we look around at the histories of systems that have succeeded in reforming themselves without external pressure, we find that innovations softened the situation and created an ethos in which new innovations were received positively.

The fact that innovations have an indirect effect on systematic reform is an important lesson to learn from other countries. Long before British primary education got reformed in the post-war efforts of reconstruction, numerous experiments had already softened the ground during the inter-war years. The experiments of Susan Isaacs or the McMillan sisters is seldom recalled now but less famous experiments are numerous. They created an ethos in which what was considered possible in the education of primary school children got stretched. Legend-making became a part of the ethos of primary education, permitting a vast body of ideas to grow, out of which a few could be institutionalized in the appropriate socio-political and post-war economic climate, when greater attention was given to education. This obviously simplified account of the British experience serves to underline the point that innovations are only steps towards reform, and are not usually directly accommodated in the mainstream.

Innovations by definition have to be short-lived, and it is this short life that has to be seen as something so stunning, and so worth preserving as a memory. Later on, when the time comes for a less radical kind of reform that might take place within the system itself, the stunning story of the innovation helps as a yardstick by which the reform effort and its performance will be judged. So one need not always be too depressed when an innovation is stopped, or when it is actually destroyed. We should be prepared for the expiry date of an innovation even as we begin it, expecting no more than that its memory should remain, both oral and written. India, unfortunately, is not a land of written memories. Far too many experiments have died without leaving a written, readable record. Oral memories last with people, and when people disappear, those go. We have very few really impressive records of Shanti Niketan, and extremely few records of basic education; many people now believe that nai taleem of Mahatma Gandhi was a failure, when in fact it was a stunning success in many parts of the country. Even as a national system, it had a remarkably long life. We need to examine why it did not sustain itself even longer.

22

Learning from *Iqbal*

Nagesh Kuknoor's film *Iqbal* poses a formidable challenge to school reformers. It tells the story of an Andhra Pradesh farmer's son (Iqbal) who wants to become a cricketer. He is bright but disabled: he can neither hear nor speak. Iqbal's mother appreciates his aspiration and encourages him, but father is deeply cynical. As the story unfolds, Iqbal's younger sister provides the key support he needs as he struggles to reach his goal; the only professional help available to him being an alcoholic teacher who couldn't survive the corruption entrenched in cricket. The poetic perfection of Kuknoor's art conceals the nature and scale of the problem Iqbal iconizes, namely, the odds against rural children's educational advancement. We are accustomed to a system which lets 53 per cent of the children drop out before they complete the eighth grade and fails millions among the ones who battle on. The overwhelming majority of the dropouts are village children, but the system victimizes the urban no less, by insisting that the same shoe must fit all. Iqbal's aspiration to be a cricketer couldn't possibly have been fulfilled had he remained at school. Not just our schools, even the best of our colleges are committed to the nineteenth-century ideal of an all-rounder. Eccentric devotion to a single pursuit, so necessary to achieve excellence, is just not accepted. Had Iqbal remained at school, he would have been forced to get through the twelfth grade with Physics, Chemistry, and Mathematics (PCM), Physics, Chemistry, and Biology (PCB), or Commerce, and it is not hard to imagine what his fate would have been.

The film makes a short mention of his rural parents' inability to afford sending him to a school for children with special needs. The fact is that even in urban centres, such schools are rare, and ordinary schools have a long way to go before they can serve children like Iqbal in an inclusive environment which brings the best out of everyone. The kinds of investments required to equip schools to become inclusive have yet to be contemplated seriously. In teacher education institutions, as they are presently constituted, the idea of giving every trainee the experience of working with children with diverse pedagogic needs sounds futuristic. Most teacher training institutes focus on the fiction of a normal child. The pedagogic methods taught are geared towards transmitting the subject matter, popularly known as content, rather than towards observing how children with different interests and capabilities might relate to it and assimilate it into their own structures of thought. Differences of cognitive style and pace among children are simply ignored, with the emphasis being on the ability to reproduce what the teacher and the textbook say. Most schools are simply not equipped to look after children with disabilities, and teachers have no clue how such children would cope with the demanding examination system.

Iqbal's sister, Khadija (played with stunning spontaneity by Shweta Prasad) is able to play a crucial role in her brother's life because she has mastered sign language although she does not need it for herself. A few weeks ago when debates on the NCF were raging, the suggestion that normal children should get a feel of Braille or sign language met with the criticism that it would increase curricular burden. Iqbal's sister reminds us why the idea is worthy of consideration. But the larger issue of burden deserves a sharp look from another angle in the context of *Iqbal*. Let us imagine that a few hundred teachers decide to take their children to a nearby cinema hall to watch *Iqbal* and then ask them to express their responses in writing or through drawing or some other medium. Someone in authority could easily see the time spent in such a project as a waste, and parents too would shout, '*Iqbal* won't get you through the board exam!'

Now that *is* true, and this is *the* problem. If something has aroused the child's interest or emotions to a high level, sustaining it at that level would require effort and time to be drawn away from routine teaching. This is something our system resists; it hates eccentricity, ignores predisposition, and punishes single-minded devotion to a particular subject at the expense of others. Education and exams seem a burden to so many precisely because everyone is assumed to be alike. The fact that many of our children excel despite the rigidities of our system encourages the popular argument that our system has rigour. Reform is resisted on the ground that our professional emigrants do so well abroad. The highly competitive character of our system inadvertently conceals a major weakness which lies in its inability to harness diversity of talent and bring the best out of everyone. A latent Darwinian streak in our socio-cultural ethos enables the system to justify a high rate of failure at every stage, starting with the primary but reaching its climax at the grade ten public examination. Any proposal to reduce exam stress is suspected to be a strategy to dilute standards. Apologists argue that stress is natural and even necessary to socialize children into the real world. To recognize that the suicidal stress our children face is a consequence of systemic malfunctioning requires a vast amount of professional awareness which decision-makers, journalists, and parents lack in equal measure. People who justify the status quo by citing the achievements of our emigrant professionals fail to notice how narrow this exported person-power is. No country can hope to build an industrial human resource by merely harnessing the cutting edge. It is the excellence of the average person that gives an industrial economy its edge. High quality leadership can hardly produce results without capable and reliable personnel to occupy the middle and lower rungs. An education system which does not allow half the child population to survive in the system long enough to move beyond grade eight cannot serve a modern industrializing economy. The talent pool from which India draws its best is so limited, yet we feel smug and defensive about our best. Imagine how much better and greater in number our best would be if they were selected from a larger pool.

Iqbal draws attention to the unjust, and not merely wasteful, character of a system which places every possible obstacle before the rural child who aspires and strives to approach the starting line. Such a system places not just children but the nation itself under stress, by reinforcing a negative, discouraging ethos. Curricular reform, which includes reduction of load, implies an attempt to make life at school more intellectually challenging, not less. And diverse too, giving ample room to the arts, heritage crafts, sports, and work-related activities. Only a comprehensive school curriculum can respond to the legitimate demand made for value-orientation. As Professor Kireet Joshi pointed out at the meeting of the CABE at which the new NCF was approved, the proposals made for art, health, work, and peace education taken together are capable of providing a strong value-orientation to the child's life at school. The new framework also makes a plea for relating teaching with children's life and learning outside, and for softening the boundaries between subjects. These ideas can help schools make classroom work more dynamic and capable of retaining children. Skeptics say that all this can't happen because good teachers are so rare. Other kinds of critics say that emphasis on child-friendly pedagogies will weaken disciplinary mastery. Still others ask: 'If exams become less stressful, how will children learn to be competitive?' Any proposal for change in education has been rightly compared to shifting a graveyard. Even the dead stand up and plead for status quo. We are lucky to have a film like *Iqbal* for it offers a crash course in psychology, sociology, and political economy of education. Those who have no time to read books and research studies can hopefully spare a couple of hours for *Iqbal*. Apart from showing how children's minds work, it also establishes that teaching is essentially a relational activity. Iqbal's strong motivation rekindles the burnt out flame of life's energy in his alcoholic teacher, played by Naseeruddin Shah, who works hard to take his pupil through the maze of middle-men while Iqbal's father is battling the new agriculture economy (that is, of genetically modified, globally marketed seeds) and bankruptcy. If *Iqbal* is shown in every school and training college, we can expect a difference in how the complex problems afflicting our system of education and lives of children are perceived.

23

Green Schools in a
Greying World

Self-analysis is a great way to learn. The CSE has applied
this idea to environment education. It organized a contest
in which schools were asked to audit their use of water,
energy, and waste control. Sharply different from the usual
song and dance one sees in the name of environment in many
schools, this contest impelled children and their teachers
to analyse the school's own track record and to improve it.
Children were expected to maintain a meticulous record of
electricity and water consumption. They were supposed to
become conscious of the daily production of waste, to weigh
it, and to bring it down. Under its Gobar Times Green Schools
programme, the CSE gave each school a manual which explains
how it can audit the consumption of natural resources like water,
land, air, and energy within its premises. Some 1,400 schools
participated in the contest, out of which twenty were shortlisted
as the greenest schools on the basis of their meticulous record-
keeping for self-audit. They were rank ordered with the help
of scores derived by rigorous monitoring of data.

Last month, when the results were declared, I felt supremely
fortunate to witness the ceremony which was like no other
I have ever seen. Records of the top twenty schools were
presented, and the excitement grew as many of the big and

famous names got cleared well before the three finalists were left. The biggest surprise came when it was announced that the first position was attained by a government school located in Boormajara village of Ropar district in Punjab. Its children and teachers could hardly believe that they had outdone so many English-medium public schools of Delhi and other cities. This school was able to attain the highest rank mainly on account of its excellent record of water recycling: it reuses 55 per cent of the water it consumes. The children collect spillage from taps and any water left undrunk in glasses to use it for washing and gardening. Second came Sholai School of Kodaikanal, which has the distinction of fulfilling its electricity requirement with the help of a micro-hydro plant, solar cells, and wind power. Inspired by J. Krishnamurti's ideals, the school participates in the National Open School examination.

In sharp contrast to these Green Schools which exemplify conscious parsimony in the use of natural resources, we now notice a growing number of wasteful schools which flaunt air-conditioned classrooms and other symbols of an extravagant lifestyle. These schools are now coming up in all parts of the country, in metropolitan as well as provincial cities, and we can hardly deny that they are setting a trend. Reflecting the lifestyle of their upwardly mobile clientele, they treat the physical infrastructure of the school as a symbol of status. Costly furniture, lush lawns, lunch packets ordered from expensive hotels, and luxury buses are used to convey the school's exclusive character. Like an expensive car or hotel, the school's name becomes an icon of privilege. It is not as if such schools deny the importance of environmental awareness. On the contrary, they flaunt special programmes and activities like bird-watching and nature walks while the everyday life and the curriculum unfold in an ethos reflecting indifference to the natural and the social milieu.

Teaching in such an ethos becomes a fractured activity, sustained by the drive to compete in national or international markets where success is measured by individual grit to pursue a narrow goal. Who can deny that this kind of goal-setting and the single-minded pursuit of wealth is an aspect of our current national ethos, not an aberration? The pursuit of wealth for its own sake had become a metaphor of national progress in the United States (US) a century ago; in India, this is happening now. *How* the nation gets rich is no longer relevant. For instance, India has now entered the global arms market as a seller and will soon have clients like Chile, Malaysia, and South Africa for its cruise missiles. The monetary gains and national pride associated with such advancements in India's industrial capacity are far too dazzling to permit us even a modicum of self-awareness. Even as we proceed towards augmenting our access to nuclear energy in collaboration with the US, we are fast developing the mindset required to ignore environmental issues associated with nuclear energy. On the water front, we are hastening towards privatization, which essentially means condemning the majority of our rural population to face a catastrophic crisis. The mobile, powerful strata have already seceded from rural India and the urban poor as far as drinking water is concerned, by accepting purified bottled water as an option to systemic availability of safe drinking water. Who bothers about the environmental effects of the millions of plastic bottles disposed off daily? Living under the delusion of 'shining India' that has now quietly reincarnated, we cannot judge how close we might be to a terrible situation even as we rush towards completing controversial projects and signing deals with predator agri-business firms.

Few though they are, CSE's Green Schools offer a modicum of hope in a schizophrenic landscape. The idea of self-audit has the potential to make environment-related learning a means of gluing back together the fragmented school curriculum. It also promises to instill mindfulness in human relations with nature and thereby materialize a dynamic kind of value education. The NCF 2005 lists several school-based reforms for which the principal and teachers are required to take the lead. The fact that in the CSE's contest a government school achieved the first rank proves that it is possible to find a creative space within the state system despite its bureaucratic routines. In the prize distribution ceremony I met children and teachers of several other government schools which could not do their best because they did not get the necessary permission and cooperation from officials. The challenge of softening the rigid administrative procedures of state directorates of education is not an easy one, and CSE will have to devise an intervention strategy. NCF 2005 suggests a number of reforms which will make government schools more flexible and capable of pursuing quality.

In private schools, the main problem is the fixation over marks. Both government and private schools have a lot to learn from institutions like the Krishnamurti Foundation, Digantar, Vikramsila, and Eklavya which have set examples of reflective pedagogy. Eklavya has recently published a Hindi translation of Ann Sayre Wiseman's classic, *The Best of Making Things: A Hand Book of Creative Discovery*.[1] This little book has made a great impact on early education in several parts of the world. The advice it gives is quite similar to Mahatma Gandhi's, but most of our teacher training institutions have closed their hearts, minds, and doors against all sources of inspiration, not just Gandhi's. If you want to find the cave where India's creative energies are locked up in abundance, all you need to do is to go to the nearest teacher training institute or college.

The Green Schools contest was based on the idea that ingenuity and activity are the heart of learning. Doing something that does not require the textbook was the main concern of the CSE. The additional parameter it should add for next year's audit is reduction in the number of the copies of the prescribed textbooks. In our system, the textbook has been used since colonial times as an axis of classroom pedagogy. It thwarts the possibility of any real linkages being formed with the world around the school. In the countries we call 'developed', teachers are trained to work with children with the help of a wide range

[1] Hand Print Press, 2005, 2nd edition.

of resources and activities. While our new textbooks go through significant reforms in approach and design, parsimony in the use of textbooks is a valid goal. For the CSE to use it as one of the parameters of a school audit makes good sense because textbook production on a mass scale by itself drains our forest resources. For an activity-centred classroom, one textbook should suffice for a group of four or five children, at least during the elementary school years. In higher classes too, our system can do with fewer copies of textbooks if the examining process is reformed in the direction of making it a part and parcel of life at school, rather than a confidential annual ritual which itself wastes a colossal amount of paper.

24

Cultural Context of
Girls' Education

If a broad profile were to be drawn of the common experience of growing up as a female in Indian society, it would highlight physical restrictions as well as mental or psychological negativity communicated to little girls from birth onwards. A son's birth is greeted with celebration while a daughter's birth is at best, endured. The unwantedness of daughters gets conveyed in ways which are hardly subtle. The idea of life-long dependence and insecurity get communicated in terms of marriage and motherhood being the sole objectives of a woman's life. The temporary nature of one's natal home and the anxiety of adjustment in an unknown family form part of the *learning* that a girl cannot escape during childhood. Communication of deep-rooted beliefs, such as the 'impurity' of menstruation, enables girls to internalize their lower ritual status under patriarchy. Transmission of culturally sanctioned attitudes constitutes the gendering process which guides girls into becoming socially acceptable women. Socialization in the family setting receives powerful reinforcement from the modern media, including both television and cinema, which use these basic elements of culture to weave commercially successful products which perpetuate tradition both in terms of its material practices and attitudes.

Little attention has been paid in educational research and teacher training to the implications of such negative aspects of girls' upbringing on their psychological development. Educational policy endorses child-centered pedagogic practices which essentially respond to the child's own search for opportunities to express agency. Nurturing of self-esteem is another major value in the child-centered philosophy of education, as it enhances the motivation and confidence to learn. In the case of girls, both agency and self-esteem come under stress and, in many cases, get damaged at an early age by behavioural practices and beliefs entrenched in the culture of child-rearing. Some of these practices have an explicitly discriminatory character, involving positive parental behaviour towards the male siblings which heightens the negative treatment meted out to girls. But even outside the frame of discriminatory behaviour, the everyday signal conveyed to girls that they have a vulnerable body and a 'weak' mind, unsuitable for the rigour of subjects like science and mathematics, poses a major challenge for school education. There is little evidence to suggest that teachers recognize the challenge or appreciate its nature and scale. They themselves carry patriarchal prejudices towards the feminine self, and in this matter, male teachers may not differ much from women teachers. Internalization of patriarchy is common to both, and teacher education does little to induce self-reflection or questioning. Teachers are trained to impart subject knowledge and that is what they mainly do, without worrying about the socially constructed structure of their students' minds.

There is then the question of the larger social milieu and its effect on girls. Little is known, for example, about how school-going girls emotionally respond to the rising incidence of female foeticide in many parts of the country, or how they interpret the aggressive behaviour of Hindu political activists which often leads to violence against young women. My own experience as a teacher suggests that girls are well aware of the deep misogyny underlying Indian societal norms. Many of them regard education as a means of acquiring greater strength to endure a social environment which is hostile to women. They expect schools and colleges to provide them with a special, positive ethos, and many institutions do make a serious effort to create such an ethos. Unfortunately, the number of such institutions is quite small, and their impact on others is insignificant. Discrimination against girls is a pervasive aspect of classroom and campus life in the overwhelming majority of educational institutions at all levels in India.

This takes many forms, some of which are entrenched in curricular and institutional policies. According to V. Geetha, as the recent studies carried out by Nirantar show, gender bias and stereotyping are not just common but structurally embedded in textbook writing, and the relatively more developed states like Tamil Nadu are no exception to this trend. The vast effort made by the National Council of Educational Research and Training (NCERT) in this respect, on the basis of the National Curriculum Framework 2005, has yet to make an impact on textbooks development processes used by state governments and private publishers. NCERT's new syllabi and textbooks take a pro-active and analytical, rather than a remedial stance towards gender asymmetry. They re-articulate social and economic relations in ways that would enable both teachers and children to notice the presence of women in social spaces where they have been rendered invisible by the symbolic power of patriarchy. For instance, in the Class VI textbook of the new subject called *Social and Political Life*, the farmer whose profile is used to draw children's attention towards the rural economy is a woman. Gender relations are introduced in other subjects and textbooks at a deeper, epistemic level, not merely to avoid the charge of bias towards women.

Such a new approach requires a revamping of the present teacher education system. Operating at the present on the margins of academic life, teacher education needs to be brought to its center. For this to happen, bridges need to be built between teacher education, on one hand, and the departments dealing with the social sciences, humanities, natural sciences and mathematics, on the other. Only an inter-disciplinary structure of study and training will allow the deep-set gender asymmetry to come under critical focus. Isolated strategies cannot be expected to go deep enough to touch the levels at which the cultural architecture of patriarchy overlaps with structures of knowledge.

Progress made towards gender parity over the recent years is quite evident in the early years of elementary education as far as enrolment is concerned. Though more girls are now attending primary schools than before and even though their numbers are comparable to those of boys in many parts of the country, the experience of the two might radically differ on account of what they have already 'learned' at home about learning. Therefore, avenues of knowledge and skill open to them may also be quite different from the ones regarded as being suitable for boys in India's growing and competitive political economy. Relevant proof of this disparity can be found in the gender break-up of entrance figures of the prestigious Indian Institutes of Technology (IITs). The proportion of girls among the successful participant in this year's joint entrance examination for IITs is just about 10 percent. This sharp disparity between the performance of boys and girls is a symbol of the multi-dimensional discriminatory regime which is culturally imposed on girls and that the system of education is unable to counter.

Girls' education needs to be looked at in a far wider and more complex and nuanced perspective than what is generally applied with reference to gender parity. This wider perspective needs to be constructed on the basis of the realization that girls' lives and education in contemporary India continue to be shaped by historical forces which have their roots in culture. The specificity of India's patriarchy lies in the relation between gender and caste. The concepts of purity and pollution are fundamental to caste, and though women themselves are deemed 'impure', the major burden of the maintenance of caste purity rests on them. According to Leela Dube, 'the principles of caste inform the specific nature of sexual asymmetry of Hindu society; the boundaries of caste and the hierarchies of caste are articulated by gender.' How caste and kinship affect girls' lives should be a matter of as much interest to the modern state as the challenges posed by the caste system to the Constitution's egalitarian social vision are. Matters pertaining to girls constitute a difficult area of social policy, and the state's record of dealing with such matters offers considerable signs of continuity since colonial times. The latest evidence of this continuity comes from the revised version of the act, approved by the parliament in 2006, which seeks to curb child marriage. The 1929 version mirrored a hesitant state, and so does the 2006 version. The state's capacity to deal with such matters was shaped during the colonial period in the context of the emerging relations of power between native elites and the colonizers. As Charu Gupta points out, Hindu revivalism and Hindu-Muslim separatism developed, during the late colonial period, a modern discourse of misogyny which later became part of a political ideology. This historical legacy continues to act as a resource for the symbolic violence that permits modernity and democracy to operate in conjunction with women's oppression from an early age. An engagement with the structures of knowledge and power which permit this conjunction to perpetuate itself is necessary to devise new policies and strategies for girls' education.

25

Their Universities,
Our Universities

There are four critical differences between universities of the Western world and ours. The *first* is that they do all they can, when they recruit young faculty, to make way for excellence. We do everything to block its entry. We start discouraging talent early, but a few bright youngsters manage to come up despite our best efforts. They are the ones who face the greatest resistance from our institutions at the time of selection for vacancies. The norms and standards that Western institutions apply for selecting young faculty focus on individualized assessment of potential. Senior people and administrators who make decisions make sure that aspirants are assessed on the basis of what they have published, the quality of research they have done, and how passionate they seem about the pursuit of knowledge and teaching. In our case, the initial criteria applied are purely mechanical. Any hint of trans-disciplinary interest means that the candidate loses the chance to be interviewed. And those who somehow escape this fate are ultimately sized up at the time of interview in terms of the lobbies they might belong to. Someone rare enough to be independent of personal as well as intellectual lobbies is the first to be eliminated. In the semi-final act of short listing, those lacking support from the dominant lobbies get weeded out. Then, in the ultimate moment, hard bargaining takes place and the institution's future gets sealed. If there is someone with an unusual background or achievement, you can depend on the selection committee to find a technical ground to reject this candidate. The only way he or she might get appointed is if a determined vice-chancellor forces such a person in. Democratic procedures and correctness have become incompatible with respect for quality. Our universities feel comfortable with the labyrinth of eligibility norms that the University Grants Commission (UGC) has nurtured with relentless energy to issue circulars over the decades. Selection committees debate over the finest of technicalities to justify the selection of the average, allowing anyone with sheen to get stuck and lost in the maze of criteria.

The *second* major difference between our universities and the Western ones relates to the concept of teaching. We calculate teaching in terms of periods taken. The Radhakrishnan Commission had bemoaned the fact that our colleges work like higher secondary schools. More than six decades after the commission gave its report, life in our undergraduate colleges is just the same. The UGC demands eighteen periods of teaching per week from an assistant professor. 'Isn't that reasonable?', one might ask. Of course, it is, if you ignore what the word 'teaching' means. The practice of calculating teachers' daily work by counting the number of periods they stand beside the blackboard exposes the hollowness of our system and concept of education. It also shows how little we have progressed since colonial days when accountability was tied to crude measures. How far Britain has moved away from the procedures it introduced in India long ago became apparent to me a year ago when I was invited to serve on a course evaluation committee in a British institute. After examining the course content, the recommended readings and the description of each lecture-session taken through the year, the committee met groups of students from the previous three years. We also read the detailed feedback each student is required to give at the end of each course. Our discussion with students and—separately--with their teachers was frank and detailed. We learnt how students assessed their teachers in terms of preparedness for each class, personal interest in the subject, the pedagogic strategies used to arouse interest, and not just regularity—which was, in fact, taken for granted. In India, we worry about attendance records to keep the student under pressure to attend classes that may be altogether devoid of intellectual stimulation. Despite attendance norms being stringent, there are classes without much attendance. There are also numerous cases of attendance *without* classes. An obsolete system of examination helps teachers who miss classes and make no effort to relate to students. There are many who take the number of periods required, but their classes have no soul or spark.

The *third* critical difference between life in an Indian university and a university in the West arises out of the concept of knowledge embedded in the system. The crude measures our regulatory bodies like UGC apply in the name of accountability mask the epistemic sterility of the curriculum, the pedagogic process and examination. In the West, curriculum and pedagogy both follow the teacher's own research interests. Even smaller universities with limited resources attempt to cultivate a research environment. Topics of research reflect the university's concern for the social and natural world surrounding it. Research is seen as inquiry to solve problems as well as to induct the young into a community of inquirers. Keeping a record of hours spent on direct teaching becomes irrelevant in such a system, even in the case of undergraduate students. To keep their research interests alive and popular, senior professors engage with young undergraduates who bring fresh questions and perspectives to ongoing inquiries. In India, you stop teaching undergraduate classes as soon as you attain professorial status. Teaching and research are seen as two separate activities. While teaching is perceived as institutional work, research is viewed as a personal agenda for moving forward in one's career. Not surprisingly, infrastructure and administrative procedures that might facilitate research do not exist. Obstacles do, and the teacher who makes the mistake of initiating a research project has to struggle all the way to its completion and the ritual of report submission to the funding agency. No one among colleagues or in the administration cares to know the findings, let alone their implications. Teaching goes on following the grooves of pre-set syllabi, like the needle boring into an old gramophone record.

The *fourth* critical difference lies in the library. In the West, even in the most ordinary universities, the library forms the centre of life, both for teachers and students. Librarians enjoy a high status as their contribution to academic life cuts across academic disciplines. They work closely with teachers and students in the various tasks involved in procurement of books and journals, keeping the library quiet and friendly, and ensuring speedy access. Our case is the opposite. The library exists on the margins of the classroom. In many universities, undergraduate students are not allowed to use the university library. Subscription to journals and magazines has dwindled over the years, and maintenance of past volumes is now seen as an obsolete practice because e-storage is available. We forget that the library is not merely a service; it is also a physical space whose ethos induces the young to learn the meaning of belonging to a community of scholars. Our reading rooms carry an unkempt, hapless look, with clanking ceiling fans and dog-eared books waiting to be picked up by daily wagers and removed. Book acquisition has been saturated with petty corruption and a crowd of spurious publishers has thrived on the outskirts of the academia.

These four critical differences are, of course, symptomatic of deeper problems entrenched in structures that govern higher education in India. Those who perceive all problems in financial terms miss the barren landscape of our campuses. Inadequacy of funds is, of course, worrisome, but it cannot explain the extent to which malice, jealousy and cussedness define the fabric of academic life in our country. There is a vast chasm that separates the Indian academia from society. Let alone the masses, even the urban middle class cares little for what goes on inside classrooms and laboratories. The citizenry does not see higher education as an intellectual resource. Nor do political leaders. The only commonly understood purpose that the system of higher education serves is to alleviate—and keep under tolerable levels of discomfort—what the British economist Ronald Dore has called the 'Diploma Disease' in his 1976 classic on education in developing economies. Dore has explained why a country like ours will continue to lag behind the West in knowledge and technique so long as we keep using mark-sheets and certificates to screen the young for further education and employment. His insight that the valid goal of widening the pool of talent is defeated by bureaucratization of selection continues to be pertinent across the colonized world.